to be of use

to be of use

the seven seeds of meaningful work

DAVE SMITH

NEW WORLD LIBRARY
NOVATO, CALIFORNIA

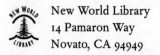 New World Library
14 Pamaron Way
Novato, CA 94949

Interior design by Tona Pearce-Myers

Library of Congress Cataloging-in-Publication Data
Smith, Dave, 1942 July 19–
To be of use : the seven seeds of meaningful work / Dave Smith.
    p. cm.
  Includes index.
ISBN-13: 978-1-57731-490-5 (hardcover : alk. paper)
1. Success in business—Religious aspects. 2. Work—Religious aspects.
3. Professional ethics. I. Title.
HF5386.S674 2005
650.1—dc22   2005014381

First printing, October 2005
ISBN-10: 1-57731-490-5
ISBN-13: 978-1-57731-490-5

♻ Printed in Canada on 100% postconsumer waste recycled paper

g A proud member of the Green Press Initiative

Distributed by Publishers Group West

10   9   8   7   6   5   4   3   2   1

For my wife, Bev,
and our sons, Josh and Aaron

My only anxiety is what I can do...could I not be of use and good for something?... The world only concerns me in so far as I feel a certain debt and duty towards it and out of gratitude want to leave some souvenir in the shape of drawings or pictures...to express sincere human feeling.

— Vincent van Gogh

Trust that which gives you meaning and accept it as your guide.

— Carl Jung

contents

introduction

This is a book about our work and our business. It's about values and meaning, ideals and responsibility, spirit and hope, creativity and community. American culture has evolved from a pioneering agrarian culture, with lots of smallholdings and local shops, into a business culture dominated by giant corporations. We are all deeply involved in the business of business as we sit at our computers, create our art, write our books, and teach our classes. Business methods, practices, and values (or the lack thereof) so dominate our lives that it is hard to imagine what people valued and how they felt in past cultures based on survival, war, religion, or fishing. One hundred years ago 90 percent of our population was self-employed. That's now been reversed: today 90 percent of the gainfully employed in the United States work in organizations.

Because we find ourselves in a culture defined by business, it is at work, and in our work, that most of us define ourselves and become who we are. I was still in high school when I got my first job — working part-time for a bank. To escape the humid heat of south Florida, where I grew up, I wrote on the job application that I wanted to work in a bank or insurance company or "any office with air-conditioning." Thus, the data processing department of the First

National Bank of Miami launched my business career, eclipsing my dad's wishes that I follow him into the ministry.

We businesspeople are sometimes heroes of our culture, with college kids madly rushing for their MBAs in order to emulate us. At other times we take our places beside the used car salespeople, the lawyers, the politicians, and the stock market analysts as the least trusted people in America, people without values or scruples, out to make a greedy buck stealing widows' savings.

I stayed in business not just to make a buck but to make a difference, not just to make a living but to make a life. I was a businessman during the sixties when my buddies shunned anything to do with business. I was a businessman during the seventies when the economy sucked and business was being blamed. I was a businessman during the eighties when business was cool, dude. I was a businessman during the nineties when everyone was clamoring to computerize the universe and get their first million by age thirty. Now it's a new century. The rot and lack of values at the center of big business have been exposed, high-profile businesspeople are in court and going to jail, and yes, I'm still a businessman.

Early on in my professional career, I realized that working for large corporations in a narrow technical specialty didn't suit me, and I gravitated to working in, creating, and turning around small businesses. At the same time, the narrowly circumscribed religion I grew up in lacked the openness and acceptance of other beliefs that I wanted to explore and understand, and I began searching for and finding common values available from the wide spectrum of wisdom traditions and religions that come to us from many cultures.

This values search began a progressive change in me. First I left a Christian Bible school to attend a community college to broaden my technical skills. There, I was elected president of the Young Christian's Club and led demonstrations in suit and tie against long-haired Vietnam protesters. Only weeks later, in maybe my life's most defining turning point, I joined those very protesters as chair of the Peace and Social Action Committee of the local Friends Meeting (the Quakers). When my father, an extremely conservative fundamentalist minister, questioned my choices, I explained that I was sincerely trying to live the values taught by Jesus in the Sermon on the Mount. My values hadn't really changed, only my understanding and application of them to changing times. I eventually quit my job in computer systems development, sold my Porsche, and began working with Cesar Chavez and the United Farm Workers Union for room, board, and five dollars a week.

As my search led me to realize, the simple core values in our own Western religious traditions are consistent with the simple values of the other great religious traditions once the obscurities added to them through the centuries — of theology, doctrine, dogma, and politics — have been peeled away to expose the true heart at their centers. Many others have pointed out that the world's religions are all remarkably consistent. Their mystics, their truly wise, share common understandings and humbly deny any exclusive access to truth. Universal spiritual principles, called by some the "perennial philosophy" and "ancient wisdom," are still our best, most basic guide to values and meaning, whether our philosophy of life is religious, spiritual, or secular.

Religions were formed out of ancient wisdom, with codified principles and commandments, but the wisdom itself was gained and passed along before there was a Confucius, a Buddha, a Muhammad, a Moses, or a Jesus to build religions around. Ancient values, advanced through millennia of human experience and inner searching and lived by the wise and caring of all eras, are timeless. They continue to help people get along with others, and they anchor our shared agreements as we find our ways through this life together. This wisdom continues to evolve and is progressively redefined as we live our lives and examine why we are here.

So what does this have to do with business and work? Only everything. Over the past few centuries, many in the West have abandoned orthodox, institutionalized religion, replacing it with scientific materialism as the basis for understanding life. In the process, we've lost much of the traditional understanding and unspoken agreements that gave life value and meaning. Economics became "the dismal science" when it abandoned anything social, psychological, or spiritual — what was meaningful — because it could not be measured. During the parallel process of industrialization that scientific materialism fostered, the value of people and our work became just another abstract economic commodity to be manipulated by the clever and powerful — the schemers, the bean counters, the bottom-liners — without any attention to the impact on our hearts, our humanity, our communities, and this precious planet we share. For many, God died. Others chose a god that could be used as an excuse for how they lived and made decisions, and they got the god they deserved. And for many, the Golden Rule, fundamental to all religions, was lost. Our sense of meaning and the values that provide meaning were lost. We lost our souls.

Losing our religion is no excuse for being irresponsible and self-centered. The values that make a good Christian or a good Buddhist also make a good citizen, a good politician, and a good businessperson. They also make a good organization and a good business. Secular values based in responsibility are just as important to maintain as religious values. And they come from the same source: wisdom traditions developed from human experience over eons. After all, the Golden Rule did not originate in the New Testament but in the sayings of Confucius, centuries earlier than Christianity. No one owns exclusive rights to religious, spiritual, or cultural wisdom and values. They've been there from the beginning. We can find good values to nourish our souls in a fortune cookie, a good book, or a holy book, and they can all help provide the foundation for a good and healthy life. We can find them all around us and deep within our own hearts.

During the social upheavals of the sixties and seventies, theories about work and livelihood took a new turn toward "enlightened management." Psychologist Abraham Maslow's theories of the *hierarchy of needs* and *peak performance* were expanded on by Douglas McGregor, who showed that authoritarian workplaces are inefficient and less profitable than those with more progressive, democratic management practices. These ideas challenged the mechanistic theories and hierarchical management principles of Frederick Taylor, which had reigned supreme since the turn of the century and have now been refuted. Taylor was quoted as saying: "In the past the man has been first; in the future, The System must be first." Contrarily, numerous studies over the past thirty years have well proven that workplaces based on trust in human nature, self-responsibility, teamwork, and values are more successful and profitable than autocratic, rigid hierarchies and mechanistic systems. These more human ways of organizing business are based on wisdom traditions and democratic principles. Yet the mechanistic and hierarchical continue as if the research, values, and principles hardly matter.

I treasure the fundamental values of the wisdom traditions — whether they come from the West, the East, the North, or the South. The wise range across history with their quiet understandings, constantly beckoning with their words and lives, surviving within larger systems often uninterested in their "quaint" search for truth. Their values are formed from the patterns of nature, learning from experience, and from loyalty to the spirit within. Wisdom and values may seem to disappear now and then, hooted down by the shallow, the crass, the venal, the grasping. But always there are those who follow a different understanding about our lives together here and what they mean.

We can bring good values and meaning to our daily work and solve basic human problems for the good of all by creating meaningful businesses and business relationships. Gandhi said: "Be the change you want to see in the world." Where we see things in business we don't like, we can be part of the solution by choosing how and where we work, and by creating the work ourselves. It is a choice.

Seeds of Greed

I wonder if you've been following what's been going on with the giant seed companies. Now largely owned by chemical companies, they are currently filing patents on the seeds that nature has provided all of us. They seek to prevent farmers from freely using them, growing more seeds with them, or passing them along to others, as peasants and gardeners have done for countless centuries. The only legal way to obtain them will be to purchase them from the seed company now claiming monopoly ownership. The company with a patent on a certain type of seed inserts a brand marker in the seeds' DNA to identify them, and if you're caught with the same species of seed without the marker, or with seeds that have the marker but no proof of purchase, then you are sued and can be thrown in jail for property theft.

A similar thing seems to be happening with our values. Like the seeds, these values originate in antiquity and have been passed along for generations. They are now being branded and ownership is being claimed by adherents of particular religious and political factions in our culture. Along with the claimed ownership is the apparent exclusive right to define and interpret how these values are to be lived. What price will be required if we don't conform to their branded definition?

That doesn't work for me, or for many others in our culture who feel our values have been misappropriated dishonestly. And there are a lot of us. We as a group hold values of peace, human rights, economic justice, clean and safe foods, sustainability, political honesty, personal responsibility, resource conservation, and positive social change. We brought "authenticity" to the marketplace, to replace the cheap and the fake. We prefer organic and natural foods and well-crafted tools. We believe in holistic and alternative health care. An underlying concern for the health of the Earth informs our decisions. We tend to be innovators and opinion leaders. We are not only from the baby boom generation but range across all ages. We are churchgoers and secularists, Republicans, Democrats, and Greenies, and we represent an alternative to the culture war between the "traditionalists" and the "moderns" that has existed in our nation from its founding. Many in this group from my own generation participated in the counterculture of the sixties and seventies, which came out of the peace movement, which itself had evolved from several hundred years of Quaker and Mennonite tradition.

We agree that we are in a crisis that threatens all life and our children's future. Earth First's Dave Foreman has said: "All of us alive now are the most important human beings who have ever lived, because we're determining the future, not just for a hundred years, but for a billion years."

According to a recent *State of the World* report by the Worldwatch Institute, we have only one or perhaps two generations to rescue ourselves. On the hopeful side, the report says that renewable energy technologies have now developed sufficiently to supply the world. These technologies could significantly reduce the threat from pollution and global warming. But currently there is a lack of political will to introduce them fast enough, even though, as pointed out by columnist Molly Ivins, 70 percent of Americans support a drastic increase in government spending on renewable energy sources, and 90 percent support a goal of energy independence.

Because we live in the richest, most powerful nation on Earth, which sometimes strays from our widely admired ideals, we are nothing less than the hope of the world right now. This is our gig whether we like it or not. You and me. Together.

Seven Seeds

The traditional idea of being "virtuous" is, unfortunately, securely tied to moralistic bigotry. The seven "cardinal virtues" as formulated by the early Christian church — faith, hope, justice, temperance, prudence, courage, and love — need updating for the world we now live in. To be virtuous is to be "good," which defines our morality and our values, and in a democracy, no one owns the exclusive right to define for the rest of us what is good, what is virtuous behavior, or to impose their definition on us. We all get to define it and "be good" together.

The seven virtues are principles for how to live wisely. They are lived as *values in action* that expand on the Golden Rule of treating others the way we would want to be treated. They come not from obligation but from personal responsibility, chosen freely, for our shared life on Earth. These virtues inform the seven seeds of meaningful work that this book is built around.

Seeds, like eggs, are self-contained embryos that hold the future. The way we go about our lives reveals the values we believe in and act on. Those values come out of who we are inside, our character, the virtues of our souls that respond to the wisdom traditions. The scripture verse "by their fruits you will know them" says it pretty well.

Take faith. Blind, rigid, unquestioning, intolerant religious faith causes division and war — my one true faith against your obviously false faith. But our faith can also be in the miracle of life and the meaningfulness of our own life and work. We can have faith that answers will appear when we need them. Faith can be an action of the heart, rather than a commitment to a narrow, exclusionary theology or reliance on those authority figures who espouse it. Faith can be trust in the good of humanity, a faith in each other, an opening of our hearts to our essential goodness. Rather than a "leap of faith," which implies the suspension of our common sense, it can be a reasonable hope that calls for the deepest and dearest and clearest truths we know within ourselves. And ultimately, only a faith acted upon is useful and valuable.

Meaning comes most naturally when we find and fulfill our purpose. This implies that there is an overall higher purpose, one beyond simply surviving and satisfying our own selves on what someone once called our separate little islands of commodities. We find our purpose in responsibility and service to others, living our values — making things better, fairer, happier for others.

At the beginning of this new century, "others" now surely means "others the world over." We can no longer pretend to be isolated from the world's troubles, or from the impact our individual daily choices have on others half a world away, or on generations to come.

Most of us live by good, solid, personal values, and most of us take personal responsibility for our actions. Our values may come from our religious faith, our spiritual understanding, or our common sense. We have high expectations of ourselves. So shouldn't we also expect our neighbors, our business leaders, and our politicians in our democratic society to have good values and take responsibility, as we do? Or are we naive to expect companies and governments to abide by the same personal values that good people, good citizens, accept as commonsense ways to get along?

In a democracy, we control the government through our elected representatives, and the government acts as our agent to control business enterprise. It was good men with decent values (for their time and place) who threw off the oppression of a foreign government and, with their idealism and hope for the future, created our democratic government based on these values. Why, then, shouldn't we expect decent values, and fair decisions based on them, from our corporate and governmental leaders? Corporations in our legal system are granted the same rights as people. Shouldn't we expect them to live up to our shared personal values? Why are so many not doing so? Why are we not holding them personally responsible?

Values Shared

We each have resources for building our own unique set of values, such as personally meaningful books. We can build rewarding value systems from the traditional wisdom found in books, ancient and modern, holy and unholy, that speak to our hearts and help us understand why we are here and how best to live and work. We may return to a few of these again and again for wisdom, comfort, and support. You'll find some of their wisdom scattered throughout this book and referenced in the bibliography. They have helped shape the values and character of our times. Through reading these works, I began to question, and by questioning, I learned how others have found answers and created wisdom. Books saved me.

Another way we find meaning is through *values-added work*. Rather than simply "adding value" to make our output more "valuable," we can become more conscious of the context of our work and of its impact, positive or negative, on other people and places. As expressed in the idea of the "triple bottom line" advocated by many progressive organizations today, *environmental sustainability* and *social responsibility* can be incorporated with a company's financial bottom line. It's true that this is often simply "greenwashing" the real way a business operates, paying only lip service to ideals or trying to fend off bad publicity with "spin." But the urgent responsibility of business now is to truly incorporate meaningful democratic values into the fabric of everyday processes and into the daily working lives of its management and employees. The consciousness and integrity of a company practicing democratic values can capture the imagination of employees, influencing the personal values of everyone involved — and lead to a more profitable, responsible, meaningful workplace.

Another way to find meaning is by looking to what I call *Creative Action Heroes* — those lives that affect our hearts and times with their "love in action." They are our contemporaries, peers, and friends who live their values — the people we look to for inspiration. Among your Creative Action Heroes might be the greengrocer on the corner. Or perhaps someone you work with, a close personal friend, a spouse, or a grandparent. Other people's active, *lived values* in their work and businesses can provide inspiration and guidance beyond, and more personally, than what we find in books. Whenever people marry their values and their ideals with their daily work, meaningful work reaches its promise. Such people are our true cultural heroes, creating a quiet revolution one life, one small business, one small farm at a time. In the epilogue you will find one way to celebrate the lives of these local heroes.

The poet William Blake said that our imagination is the part of us that is most sacred. Einstein said that imagination is more important than knowledge. Buckminster Fuller said that if we are not full of imagination, we aren't very sane. I'm hopeful because I can still *imagine* hope — and I can only imagine hope because I know people who work tirelessly and creatively to make a positive difference in the world despite a careless and often uncaring culture. Hope and meaning come alive when someone takes responsibility for being useful. Those making a positive difference embody hope itself. Hope imagines a future that is meaningful, work that has purpose, and the creative use of our hearts and intelligence.

As a businessman and a human being, I treasure meaningful work and meaningful workplaces. A reformation of values in our work and businesses could help reform the values in our larger culture and the world we live in. I honor the lives of those many, many unsung heroes around us who haven't shuffled into line along the easy routes, but have struck off into the future to carve out their unique and inspired paths against all odds, living and working quietly, without fanfare, heroically, meaningfully. It is here that I find hope, embodied and shining. You may be one of them. Some of them you may know. A few you will meet here.

They make all the difference for me.

to be of use

The people I love the best
jump into work head first
without dallying in the shallows
and swim off with sure strokes almost out of sight.
They seem to become natives of that element,
the black sleek heads of seals
bouncing like half-submerged balls.

I love people who harness themselves, an ox to a heavy cart,
who pull like water buffalo, with massive patience,
who strain in the mud and the muck to move things forward,
who do what has to be done, again and again.

I want to be with people who submerge
in the task, who go into the fields to harvest
and work in a row and pass the bags along,
who stand in the line and haul in their places,
who are not parlor generals and field deserters
but move in a common rhythm
when the food must come in or the fire be put out.

The work of the world is common as mud.
Botched, it smears the hands, crumbles to dust.
But the thing worth doing well done
has a shape that satisfies, clean and evident.
Greek amphoras for wine or oil,
Hopi vases that held corn, are put in museums
but you know they were made to be used.

The pitcher cries for water to carry
and a person for work that is real.

— Marge Piercy

faith

[true belief]

The miraculous is not extraordinary but the common mode of existence. It is our daily bread. Whoever really has considered the lilies of the field or the birds of the air and pondered the improbability of their existence in this warm world within the cold and empty stellar distances will hardly balk at the turning of water into wine — which was, after all, a very small miracle. We forget the greater and still continuing miracle by which water (with soil and sunlight) is turned into grapes.

— Wendell Berry

Religion is something you do, not something you believe.

— Kenneth Rexroth

I wonder if you've ever experienced an epiphany — a sudden, emotional, unexplainable understanding, a "peak experience" that delivers you suddenly, powerfully, and immediately into the present. Epiphanies have been described as an awakening, a feeling of wholeness, an illumination, a mystical relation to the infinite — the feeling that everything is just right and well and as it should be. Similar experiences of oneness with all have been felt by basketball players in the swirling midst of an important game when everything just "clicks," by Sufi dancers twirling together in spiritual ecstasy, by jazz players riffing off tight grooves in small combos, by holy rollers babbling in a language no one understands.

I once had such an experience — while working in a grocery store.

Epiphany under the TP

In the mid-seventies, with the Vietnam War winding down and the economy in shambles with high unemployment, I helped some friends start up and run a small, cooperative natural food store in Menlo Park, California. An abandoned 7-Eleven on a frontage road near a freeway was transformed into the Briarpatch Cooperative Market, associated with the legendary Bay Area small business community known as the Briarpatch Network. Three of us were paid to comanage the store, which was staffed by its member-owners. Members were required to work eight hours every three months, running the cash registers, cutting and wrapping the cheese, buying at the San Francisco produce terminal at 3:00 A.M., taking inventory, and stocking shelves. In return, we purchased natural and organic food at prices averaging 30 percent less than those at the local supermarkets and natural food stores. At one point there were 350 families on our waiting list. Our slogan: "We do it ourselves."

We were serving each other and our community with healthy food. We all owned it, we all ran it, and we all benefited from it. Our express register was for members in a hurry, who could ring up their own groceries and leave their money in the drawer. A large poster on the back wall read: "Cooperation is the fun of being and doing together."

Managing the chaos created by untrained and energetic workers along with constant interruptions by shoppers and delivery trucks was both challenging and absorbing. One could only cope by complete immersion in the activity. When it was my turn to run the swing shift, I would come in around noon and immediately dive into the work, already in full active swirl. There was no time to come up for air, to step back and calmly assess priorities. It was full absorption, snap decision making, and constant physical movement. At the end of the business day, as the last shoppers left and a member counted the till and tallied the day's sales, I would suddenly seem to arrive back into myself.

One day in the midst of this constant chaos, I was sitting in the back room at the comanager's desk, its surface covered with notes and paperwork. Overhanging the desk were shelves filled with back stocks of paper towels and toilet paper. Across the aisle was the cheese-cutting table, and next to that, a member was washing produce in the sink. Another member had just gone into the walk-in refrigerator to restock the dairy case. I distinctly remember the song playing on the radio — "...good lovin' is all I really need, c'mon now and gimme some of that good good lovin'" — and the nearby member waiting to unload the next delivery truck was most likely boogying to the music. I looked up from my paperwork and suddenly there was a pause. Everything stopped and all was silent. In one brief moment I experienced what is. In a flash I seemed to meld into and become this open, caring community of hope and love and giving together. I was overwhelmed with a feeling of wonder at the mystery and beauty of it all. The chaos was transformed into a meaningful, joyful, unchoreographed dance, frozen in time. In that moment I felt that I would be completely consumed by emotion coming up from somewhere very deep. If my overcivilized ego had not immediately stepped in to roughly grab hold and shove it back down my throat, I think I would have sobbed for hours. Even as I sit here now at my laptop describing it to you many years later, the memory threatens to emotionally engulf me once again.

All we really need is some of that good, good lovin'. Why are such life-affirming experiences so rare? In the midst of our everyday work, we may give pause and wonder why so much of it is love-*less*, meaning-*less*.

Counter Cultured

Once upon a time, members of my generation broke free and created what was labeled a "counterculture." Because the surrounding culture was not living up to our young ideals, we began creating our own work, our own services, our own communities. I prefer to call what many of us were doing a "parallel culture," as my experience was more about building something new rather than countering or opposing. Between the straight culture and the anticulture, we chose to be part of a third way, seeking to build something positive out of the chaos rather than just spending all our time protesting and demonstrating. We chose to compose new social and workplace structures and relationships, *practicing* and *feeling* them, discovering how to make them meaningful and how to restore a measure of love and joy and amazing grace to our daily work. Instead of remaining within rigid hierarchies and stratified gender roles, we were all in it together. Sure, we made mistakes, but we were willing to fail young rather than take our assigned places and nod off into the ethical and moral wasteland we found around us.

Those times in the sixties and seventies mean different things to different people, and our memories of that time are most often associated with events and places. One image we have is Woodstock: free lovin', dope smokin', skinny-dippin', screw-it-all, hippie heaven. Another is Berkeley: radical, peacenik, burn-it-down, antiwar, antinuke, anti-everything. Another is the Summer of Love in the Haight-Ashbury of San Francisco in 1967. At the time, I was coming of age in the center of it all, in the San Francisco Bay Area, where I migrated after having grown up in south Florida, a land of racial segregation with its separate schools, separate restaurants, and separate public water fountains marked "Colored" and "White."

Along with many others, I had responded to John F. Kennedy's call to service. We believed we could and would change the world, and we did. Along with our protests and marches for civil rights, farmworkers' contracts, and the environment, we organized free universities, cooperative food stores, and small alternative community businesses. Our memories of that time are overwhelmingly positive. We had passionate faith in the future and look back now with pride at our accomplishments. We stopped a war. We put civil rights into law. We shut down the building of new nuclear plants. We passed the Endangered Species Act, the Clean Air Act, the Clean Water Act, and the National Environmental Policy Act — every one of them now being chipped away by the culture that was then being countered. We created movements built around human potential, women's rights, the environment, alternative health, and natural foods. Many of the positive results have by now been diffused into the overall culture as part of our everyday lives. One of many examples is the market for organic foods. The demand for healthy foods germinated in the fifties through vitamin-centered health food stores and a few scattered organic farms and took root in the sixties through hippie cooperative buying clubs and the popularity of Asian diets. The organic food market has now been growing over 20 percent per year and has gone mainstream.

For me, the sixties and seventies were *not* about selfishness and doing our own thing, an interpretation that has been perversely sensationalized by the media. Those years were delightfully exuberant with passion, idealism, possibility, higher vision, and work from the heart. They were a way out of the suffocating soullessness imposed by a scientific materialist worldview, the conformity that corporate mega-machine behaviorism requires, and the individualistic selfishness hyped by its marketing. Alienated by the rugged cowboy models of isolated, independent manhood, many of us practiced tribal values of mutual aid and support, the common good in community, and the use of our gifts and creativity for others. We relearned how to take responsibility for each other, have faith in each other, help each other, care about each other, share with each other, cooperate with each other — values that have kept cultures together since humankind began. We were lighthearted and joyous in our abilities to live simply and walk lightly on the Earth. We worked hard at what we believed in and had an enormous amount of fun doing it. Our daily life glowed with purpose and meaning, and we believed deeply what one of the Beat writers, Jack Kerouac, had written: that without feeling and emotion, nothing can really be *known*. He was echoing Thoreau, who said that a person has not really seen a thing who has not felt it. Or, as Janis Joplin famously sang: "You know you got it if it makes you feel good."

As budding businesspersons, we were inspired and energized by the psychologist Abraham Maslow and management professor Douglas McGregor. Maslow wrote that personal salvation is a by-product of self-actualizing work and self-actualizing duty, and that the proper management of the work lives of human beings can improve them and improve the world. McGregor, who based much of his work on Maslow's research, portrayed managers as either authoritarian on the one hand, or collaborative and trustful of people on the other. Their published research proved that cooperative democratic principles applied to business management not only created better places to work but were also more profitable — that managers who were compassionate, helpful, friendly, altruistic, and democratic always produced better results. Maslow wrote that the "best way to destroy democratic society would be by way of not only political authoritarianism but of industrial authoritarianism, which is anti-democratic in the deepest sense."

What was the context that led us to attempt new lives and livelihoods during the Cold War with the Soviet Union and the "hot war" in Vietnam? We had grown up cowering under our school desks during air raid drills, preparing for potential nuclear annihilation. Friends were leaving, fighting, and dying, and for who knew what? We knew there must be a better way to run the world, and it had to start by remaking the "lethal culture" of our elders.

But we lost our way. The giant corporate MegaMaw lifted its ugly head from its ceaseless devouring, looked us straight in the eye, and said, "No you don't" (see chapter 5). We did anyway...for a while. But we were soon devastated by the deaths of progressive political leaders, brought down so suddenly and shockingly, and we were left lamenting what could have been. The Vietnam War dragged on as the positive and creative alternatives gave way to deep divisions and antagonism. Many of us gave it all up to despair, drugs, and deluded insurrections. And in our confusion we took the easy way out and lost ourselves by moving back into what the institutions of our culture had planned for us all along: safe careers, cake and circuses, bright shiny chariots, and commutes to tall buildings. Sure, you could say that we were on the losing side of the culture wars, or you could say it was simply time for us to grow up, move on, raise our families, and take our places of responsibility. Many of us turned inward, feeling that the only real change is spiritual and psychological, and that what is important is personal growth. But personal growth without an eventual return to the scene of the crimes to take up compassionate action is only escape into navel-gazing denial and the postponement of personal and social defeat. The goal is not *either/or*, it's *both/and*. It takes both personal growth and social involvement to live the purposeful, meaningful life that is the fulfillment of our human potential.

I still cherish the traditional values we lived then. We were on to something, with great creative, stumbling, desperate leaps into anything that was better, more life affirming. Those values derive from old-fashioned, responsible, conservative ideals that promote community service, spiritual understanding, mutual cooperation, and democratic decision making. And they didn't lose their hold on us. Instead of giving up on those values, I realized, along with many others, that it was going to take longer to see them bear fruit. A stubborn patience, an unwavering faith, a clear hope were going to be required, and we hunkered down for the long haul.

Finding and Creating Meaningful Work

Since those inspiring but disappointing days, many of us have incorporated those values and experiences into our careers and companies. The more celebrated successes have included Ben and Jerry's, The Body Shop, and a whole slew of companies involved with natural and organic foods, like Whole Foods Market. To establish my own credentials for writing a book like this, please allow me to briefly list what I've been up to these past few years.

The following describes most of the companies I've been personally involved with while practicing my own vocation. Each was organized to solve a social problem. They defined and held a sense of mission, even in the face of real-world, rough-and-tumble business enterprise. Some continue to be successful; some were successful for a while. I had various responsibilities within these companies, and in all cases it was a privilege and a joy to be a part of them.

Briarpatch Cooperative Market

The Briarpatch Co-op was created in the mid-seventies during difficult economic times and high unemployment to provide natural and organic food at more affordable prices. Local health food stores were expensive and many people had time on their hands, so the Briarpatch was established as a cooperative membership market. Members were provided with traditional groceries along with natural and organic foods. After I had moved on and the economy improved, members began finding work again. The staff's wages began rising along with prices, sales declined, and the store stopped making economic sense. It eventually closed down. All investment was returned to its members, all vendors were fully paid, and a joyful, successful community business had run its course. A social problem had been solved by a cooperative business. This has been the history of cooperatives generally, especially during hard times: a need is not being met well in the community, so the community members band together and create a solution themselves.

Smith & Hawken

I cofounded this company in 1979 because more and more organic farmers did not want to use pesticides and large tractors to farm with, but rather were relying on smaller rototillers and hand tools to cultivate and weed. Hand tools such as shovels and garden forks then being produced for home gardeners would break when brought into the more vigorous application of market gardening and small farming. We discovered that high-quality professional hand tools were still being used and manufactured in England. At first, importing these tools for small farmers and serious gardeners was a part-time venture, but it soon turned into a growing business that continues to this day.

My partner and I, along with our original ideals, left the company long ago. The company that owns Smith & Hawken today, Scotts, does not maintain the vision or the ideals that built the company. They are a leader in pesticide distribution and genetic engineering, anathema to small organic farmers everywhere and something I actively oppose. Sad to say, in my opinion, my company, formed to solve a social problem, has evolved into the problem. Disheartening as that may be, during its heyday, Smith & Hawken and its values helped inspire our culture in a way that hopefully endures.

SelfCare Catalog

SelfCare was a pioneer of the wellness movement, which aimed to help people take more control of their personal health. The catalog's mission was to educate individuals about their own health and to liberate the health information hoarded by the medical industry. We sold medical devices such as stethoscopes and speculums for consumer use and informed readers about natural alternatives and complements to other medical care. Libraries, bookstores, and the Internet now make health information about alternatives readily available, allowing informed choices rather than total reliance on medical experts. But back in the seventies, it was almost impossible to find much useful information. I was brought in by new investors as CEO in 1989 to turn it around. Several years after I moved on, the company got caught up in the dot-com bubble and went bust along with many others. It was then absorbed into the publicly traded company Gaiam, which espouses many of the values that the SelfCare customers hold dear. Alternatives to drugs and the traditional medical system — from acupuncture to homeopathy to yoga — are now easily available everywhere.

Real Goods

A pioneering company in renewable and alternative energy systems, Real Goods has a catalog business that promotes energy saving products to consumers. Its Solar Living Center in Hopland, California, sells and installs a full line of alternative power systems and offers educational programs on everything from straw bale home construction to the technical aspects of independent living. The center's land includes a solar energy facility that not only provides power for the store but also sells power back to the grid. Like SelfCare, Real Goods is now also owned by the Gaiam company and remains true to its mission of solving an ongoing social problem. I served on its board of directors and was also the operations executive for a while.

Seeds of Change

Founded originally in Oregon as Peace Seeds, Seeds of Change is the pioneer in producing organically grown seeds. Only recently have more organic seeds become readily available to organic gardeners and farmers, who were previously forced by lack of supply to purchase nonorganic seeds. I was brought in first as a consultant, and then in 1997 as an executive to run the catalog business and develop the website and newsletter. The company was purchased by the candy company Mars Incorporated, which wanted to get into the mushrooming organic food business and, with the best of intentions, needed a brand of authenticity to give its fledgling organic food business a solid history. Seeds of Change continues to be a successful seed and food company as part of Mars Incorporated.

Diamond Organics

Created to provide organic food to consumers who don't have ready access to local sources, Diamond Organics ships organic produce, flowers, meat, dairy products, and other organic food directly to consumers overnight via FedEx and UPS. Please see chapter 6 for more on this company. I currently serve on the board of directors, have managed operations, and headed up marketing at different times over my several years being in and out of the company.

Organic Bouquet

I cofounded this flower company in 2001 as the next step in sustainable organic agriculture. Nearly everyone understands that what we put in our mouths is important to our personal health, and that organic food is a healthy alternative to food produced by large, commercial, nonorganic growers. But fewer people understand that organic agriculture involves far more than eating for your own health. It is also about the health of farmworkers and others who live in agricultural areas, wildlife, our water supplies, our land — the environment itself. Thus, raising flowers organically takes us a step beyond thinking only about the food we eat. Among people working in the conventional flower growing industry there is a high incidence of disease caused by the chemicals used to grow these beautiful crops. Growing flowers organically greatly reduces the rates of cancer and other illnesses among these workers.

Organic to Go

This 2004 start-up was created by a friend in Seattle to provide delicious organic food, carefully prepared, for takeout and delivery to time-challenged consumers and businesses. As an alternative to fast food, notorious for its high fat, high sugar, empty calories, and indifferent preparation, this company brings the organic movement home. I'm on the founding board of directors, publish the newsletter, and work with local organic farmers who supply the company's ingredients. It is now expanding into other parts of the country, working with local organic and sustainable farmers in each area.

Mendocino Organic Network

Most recently, I cofounded the nonprofit Mendocino Organic Network to promote local small farm organic agriculture. (In chapter 6, you'll read the story of how my fellow cofounder Els Cooperrider led the first successful fight against the chemical MegaMaws to ban genetically engineered plants from Mendocino County.) We are an organization of consumers, farmers, and activists disappointed in how the government is implementing and lowering the organic standards that it has taken over to accommodate the new, large corporations getting into the market. It is costing small farmers too much time and money to do the paperwork and become certified. So we've created an organization to apply the original strict standards in our own county, and to certify farmers at a lower cost. We also promote the farmers with our own marketing and branding label.

I have also been involved in the nonprofit world, worked with autistic children, worked with Cesar Chavez in the United Farm Workers Union, and served for many years on the board of directors of Ecology Action of the Midpeninsula (south of San Francisco) and on the board of the Ukiah Natural Foods Cooperative in Ukiah, California.

Just a Guy

I'm not trying to set myself up as some self-righteous example, saying that I have faithfully lived by my values or am a purist about them. Although I've consistently tried to involve myself in useful work that makes a difference, we are all embedded in an industrial and marketing infrastructure that defines the rules of the game. Our culture's Creative Action Heroes often need to change the rules. But I'm no hero. I've made my living as a mail order cataloger, responsible for cutting down forests to paint attractive word pictures and splash fancy photographs across bleached-white, dioxin-embedded pages that 98 percent of the recipients will assign directly to the trash without opening. This is wasteful, harmful, and contradictory to my basic values. We all make short-term and long-term compromises that are inexcusable when scrutinized alongside what we believe and say our values are. I certainly admire year-round bicycle commuters, especially those who live in Wyoming or Minnesota, pedaling through sleet and snow. But I was once knocked off my bike by a motorist from behind and I'm no longer willing to make my body vulnerable to the distracted, inebriated, or drugged. So I drive a car and contribute to global warming, like most everyone else.

Still, I have confidence that together we can change the ways we live and work now to be more in tune with the habitat we have been so mysteriously and generously provided with. And it will be by working together, maybe through the businesses that we create and work in, that the greatest strides toward personal and organizational sustainability and responsibility will be made. One can hope, and one can keep the faith.

Belief Systems

I was raised in a religion born of protest — the Protestant religion created in opposition to the orthodox claim of an exclusive right to religious truth. And the branch of my upbringing is the most virulent and antagonistic of the Protestant sects — Christian fundamentalism — which claims its own exclusive right to truth. Out of that experience came my own personal search, the search of one who is sometimes lost and accepts what life offers with no ready, premade answers. I believe that out of each sincere personal search, an original sacred answer to life can be born.

My spiritual search is of no interest to you or anyone else unless we can together find common ground and mutual sympathy without imposing our own answers on each other. Organized religions come about when someone discovers his or her own unique path and conveys it to others with such complete conviction that a new belief system is built and codified by the followers. There is nothing wrong with getting together to share a belief system, as long as it is not imposed on others as the one and only truth, or incorporated as the basis for an imposed government, or enforced with violence.

Thomas Jefferson and Leo Tolstoy were so flummoxed by the contradictions and inconsistencies in the New Testament that they created their own versions of the scripture. They felt that some of the New Testament's original authors, the orthodox church, and the political powers that adopted it had added on their own interpretations and myth making and had even put words in Jesus' mouth for political reasons, distorting the real truth about his life and work and teaching. So they took up where the original authors left off, eliminated what they themselves concluded was in error through their research, and published their own versions, which they felt were more consistent with the life that Jesus apparently led. That's one way to do it, and the most current research by biblical scholars verifies their suspicions. But traditional wisdom from antiquity to the present is also available for our inspiration.

Some would have us believe that the Founding Fathers created this nation based on the Christian belief system, and that our legal system is based on that system. But these notions have now been thoroughly researched and discredited by author Thom Hartmann, among others. Our Constitution contains not a single mention of Jesus, God, Christianity, or the Bible. The "Tripoli Treaty" was officially ratified by the Senate with John Adams's signature on June 10, 1797, and it stated: "The United States is in no sense founded upon the Christian religion." Our Founding Fathers were the first liberal humanists and theists — believers in God and the innate goodness of human beings, but not in Christian doctrine or the Christian church. They insisted on a strict separation of church and state. These were the men who conducted the American Revolution and wrote the Constitution and Bill of Rights that established our government. They knew well the history of the many religious wars that had wracked Europe for centuries, the Inquisitions and witch hunting that brought hell to earth, killing millions of "heretics" and "unbelievers." They were determined to make the United States free of sectarianism and open to all religious beliefs or nonbelief. We can see the unfortunate result of imposing a god-centered ("god" here meaning someone's *concept* of God), theocratic tyranny in some Islamic countries and can thank the wisdom of Thomas Jefferson, James Madison, Thomas Paine, Benjamin Franklin, and others for their wisdom and our religious freedoms. Eternal democratic vigilance is required against inroads that any religion or ideology begins to make into our democratic government. Our freedom *of* religion can only be guaranteed by a government free *from* religion.

Wisdom Traditions

The classical Greek (pagan) philosophers considered the foremost virtues to be temperance, courage, justice, and prudence. Early Christian leaders appropriated these virtues for their own theology, calling them the "cardinal virtues" and deeming them applicable to all people, whether Christian or not.

It was Saint Paul who defined the three chief virtues as faith, hope, and love, which, he proposed, are not natural to human beings but can be conferred by Christian baptism. The early Christian Church fathers combined the cardinal virtues and the chief virtues together into the seven theological, or "heavenly," virtues, making themselves the sole self-appointed definers and arbiters of what is good and what is bad, what is virtuous and what is immoral.

Stripped of religion and doctrine, the seven virtues are simple, commonsense principles about making one's way in life and working constructively with other people to survive and thrive. If we could go way back in time, we would find their origins in the intuition, myths, stories, allegories, and simple daily living of primeval indigenous and aboriginal peoples the world over, as demonstrated by those few left to tell the tales. Sure, they may be mixed in with a heap of superstitious hooey, but the more arcane practices of our own Western religious beliefs should give one pause before looking for stones to chuck at "primitive" beliefs.

The original wisdom of the great religions was humanistic in its values and goals: teaching the betterment of humanity and placing our values and well-being above all other considerations — above the culture, above politics, above economics, above church, above the state. Jesus was not out to build a world religion; he was living, practicing, and teaching values and freedom from the cruelty and bondage to any human-made religious system or set of orthodox rules. He loathed materialism, raged against hypocrisy, and cursed the smug religious professionals who twisted basic values into a self-serving, rigid system of do's and don'ts — those who loved telling everyone what they were doing wrong, even while cozying up to the corrupt, oppressive, occupying Roman political powers. He disdained the religious and political establishment of his time, calling the Pharisees (the religious right and Puritans of his day) "liars" and "hypocrites." So he introduced a more truthful, egalitarian value system based on traditional wisdom, organized some of his buddies together to practice and promote the daily living of those values, and paid the ultimate price for being an outspoken radical progressive. The religious and political authorities of the privileged establishment were threatened because the basis of their power was being called into question. The values taught by Jesus undermined both the authorities and their authoritarianism. Since they could not co-opt or buy him off and he was seriously impeding their running of things, they had him killed to preserve their power. Jesus, representing the sacred spark within, lived for and taught values and meaning. He was explaining anew the old values already known but obscured and submerged, and updating them for the situation he found his culture in. His life reflected the seven virtues. I love him for that.

Of course, Judeo-Christian wisdom traditions have no exclusive lock on the truth. No one owns values. No one owns the still, small voice within, or the wisdoms handed down. Eastern religions all offer guidance based on their traditional understandings about our lives and work. Though they are infinitely different on the surface, the great Eastern and Western religions share basic, timeless values at their core. Their fundamental principles are the true natural religion that appeals to all hearts, and they are simple and easily understood.

The great religions agree that there is one God or power. (For secularists this simply means that a single force unites us all; for Buddhists it means that with which we unite when we reach Nirvana.) They agree that in each of us is a sacred spark that can either diminish or grow brighter by how we live our lives. This spark is diminished by self-love and increased by selfless love. The simple ways to increase this sacred spark into a way of living include listening to our inner voice, meditating to touch what is real, paying attention to our intuition and dreams, and proactively treating others as we would have them treat us. That is apparently the way ancient traditional wisdom was developed and passed on.

There is much to be valued in the seven virtues of Christianity without becoming tied up in culture wars or hoary theology. In fact, the seven virtues need to be set free from the grip of self-righteous self-promoters: those solemn head-shakers, finger-waggers, Bible-thumpers, and grim, holier-than-thou moralists who wish to impose their platitudinous pieties on us through guilt or brute force.

Any set of rules or code of conduct that becomes a formula is dead. Theological doctrines were formed many centuries ago to strengthen and perpetuate the power of priests and preachers. We can focus on words and descriptions and the parsing of concepts until we've lost our true goal, which I feel is to consciously know and work on ourselves *internally* so that *externally* we can truly serve humankind in whatever modest, unheralded, meaningful work may be set before us. Useful virtues should move and evolve and ask us to examine our lives in light of what is real right now. Virtues that are cast in stone, becoming a code of conduct imposed by self-righteous moralists, are not useful. Virtues are timeless but flexible enough to be reinterpreted, and adaptable enough to speak anew to each generation. They appeal across time, generations, cultures, belief systems, ethnic and religious boundaries. Buddha's last words were said to have been that each of us must work out our own salvation.

Seven Seeds

This book describes the search for meaningful work. Based on the traditional values of the wisdom traditions, this search can be a bridge from antiquity to the present, and it can form connections between the religious, the spiritual, and the secular elements of our lives. In this search we pause to examine our lives and our work and ask questions that matter: How am I doing in my life? Does my work have meaning? Based on what? How do I judge myself and my work against my own internal set of values? Am I on track, or have I lost my way? How do I judge my values and my work against the values that my culture or government or profession profess to believe in?

Are we *all* on track, or have we *all* lost our way? What is the point, or is there any point at all?

Unless we are locked into a narrow, fundamentalist, exclusionary belief system, we can accept all religious experience as having truth and can deny the obvious absurdity of the claim that any particular way is the only one and true way, a claim that is made simply because we were born into that way or because it is *our* way. As in eclectic music, progressive politics, organic agriculture, and healthy social groups, diversity is the key to exciting, healthy, creative, meaningful, and joyous community and livelihoods. All religions have parallel wisdoms we can draw from. They each contribute to universal spiritual principles, and they all share the basic values summed up by the Golden Rule and its Buddhist corollary, "loving-kindness." The wisdom of our traditional values continues to live and progress creatively in the people around us and to be articulated by the wise of the present day.

In a few moments you'll meet my dad. He was a true believer in his religion, proselytizing almost everyone he met, boldly handing out religious tracts and "winning souls for Christ." Hanging on his bedroom wall was a small plaque that read: "Only one life 'twill soon be past / Only what's done for Christ will last." If we take that idea out of a purely Christian context into the broader realm of traditional values and restate the second verse, "only what's done for *love* will last," we have a simple definition of "meaning." It faces us first with our own unavoidable demise as the context of judging what is of value. (Or, as the blues tune more colorfully puts it: "There ain't no luggage rack on a hearse.") Then the enduring value of love places meaning in the context of relationship with others. Meaning has to do with human relationships and our contribution to progressive purpose and growth in understanding and responsibility. Helping make the world a better place for us all through our work brings meaning to it.

Recently I was browsing through a *New Yorker* magazine at the bookstore when I was stopped cold by a simple cartoon showing a gravestone bearing the epitaph: "He watched sports." There's certainly nothing wrong with watching sports, and I'm not interested in passing judgment on anyone else's use of time. But it may be interesting to reflect on what others might write on our tombstone, or what one's obituary would read if a committee of friends and enemies got together to write it. For a moment, imagine you can look back at your life from two hundred years in the future. Did your work have meaning? Did you and your values count? Did they have even the slightest positive impact on humankind? Or maybe you can take a fantasized out-of-body experience and zoom up a few miles into space and observe yourself going about your daily work. Are you being useful in a meaningful way? Do you like what you see yourself doing?

Dilbert Land

Before I graduated into more fulfilling work in progressive causes and small businesses, I had advanced partway up the ladder of corporate management in computer systems. I soon realized that I was not cut out for the big corporate life I experienced around me. I felt like a vaguely robotic human, easily replaced by a vaguely humanized robot. The warm, crazy emotionalism of the small, fundamentalist church community I grew up in apparently prepared me for group behavior that was definitely lacking in the austere, formal, fluorescent, abstract, competitive environs of my first corporate jobs with a national bank, a defense contractor, and an auto distributor. It was then that I began to search for work with meaning, not really knowing what I was looking for.

The search for meaningful work begins with questions about our work that are hard to answer honestly: Do I love my work? Has my company been good to me? Or have I surrendered my soul to it for relative security, benefits, and perks? Does the company I work for help make the world a better place or a worse place to live? Do its values coincide with my own? Am I spending the precious hours of my life giving, or taking? Is my workplace conducive to spiritual epiphanies, or is my soul quietly leaking out all over the computer keyboard? What do I think of my company's management philosophy? Is it open to democratic, bottom-up decision making, or is it the usual top-down bureaucratic hierarchy? What about this idea of "management by walking around" — the tall guy with the perpetual coffee cup and smile? Does he have me snowed? Is he working? Is he managing? Hey, just what in the hell does he get paid for doing, anyway?

We no sooner get through that list of questions when more thoughts arise: Have I given up on having what I want from my work and my life? I find myself feeling a little tired of being a "human resource" rather than a human being. I've read about enlightened companies that try to find out what their employees want and need from their work and then line these up with the company's wants and needs. But will my company ever do that? Does it care about me at all?

Hard Work

I don't know about you, but I came here to work. My grandparents were peasants — farmworkers who owned small farms. The dictionary defines peasants as "unsophisticated country persons" and "farmworkers." The word "pagan" originally meant "peasant" until early Christian leaders redefined it to mean "heathen," which meant anyone who did not accept their particular religion. But I use the term "peasant" as an honorific rather than a pejorative.

My maternal grandfather was a dairy and seed farmer who emigrated with his family from Switzerland to escape orthodox religion's fierce hold on his culture. He spent the rest of his life farming in Northern California. My paternal grandfather was an Irish farmer who immigrated to Tennessee and ended up in the dust bowl of Oklahoma, trying to farm and run a bar at the same time. My father and his brother escaped Oklahoma, fleeing to California atop railroad boxcars. Although my father became a minister — a "professional" — his congregations were always a mixture of peasant class and blue-collar working-class people.

My ancestors, like many of yours, came from elsewhere because elsewhere didn't work for them. Their descendants, my family, are now shoved up against the Pacific Ocean in California, gazing into the future with nowhere else to go to find something better. There are no more escapes to new frontiers and a better life. And because there will always be those who wish to reimpose the harmful belief systems and harsh conditions our ancestors escaped from, we have no choice now but to turn, hunker down, and work for what is best where we now find ourselves.

Coming from peasant stock, I'm working-class, low caste all the way through. I'm from the dirt of the Earth, and I identify with people of the Earth. My uniform is denims — what we used to call dungarees — and pocket T-shirts purchased at the hardware store, with Converse sneakers; it's the same basic uniform I wore in junior high school, where I hung out with my low-class hoody friends. Freedom of dress has a strange hold on me. The uniform of suit and tie I donned for a few years represented selling out to "the Man." Thoreau's advice to "beware the enterprise that requires new clothes" became a measurement of my enslavement as I gazed in the mirror each morning, cinching my necktie, feeling my soul being seized by the throat. The relaxed dress standards in company offices beginning in the sixties were most welcome.

Recent peasant ancestry can often be spotted in the hands. My mom and my three sisters are pretty, soft, well-rounded, and fully female, but their hands (and mine and my brother's) are the hardworking, heavily veined, rough-fingered hands of peasants. In their teens, my mom and her siblings were out in the fields hoeing weeds and harvesting seeds before they went to school. Back in the sixties when I was contemplating a move to a commune in the country, I mentioned to my mom that I was going back to the land, thinking how proud she would be of my continuing a family tradition. She laughed and sobered me up quick: "Oh, you can have the land." I soon realized, before I made a disastrous career move, that I was more an armchair farmer than a dirt farmer.

Looking at the sophistication and technical skills that we may have attained, we have to ask, what sort of people are *needed* on Earth? Who are the self-sufficient, the independent? Who are skilled at *growing* and *harvesting* the food that keeps us all alive? Who knows how to *build* a roof over their heads rather than just *buying* one? Who knows how to *make* clothing rather than simply *shopping* for it? Who are really the *needed*, and who are really the *needy*?

In developing countries, peasants have been forced off their own land and are reduced to working someone else's land or cross the border and hand us our food from computer-programmed frying systems. In the process of "fencing the commons" that has been going on now for several hundred years in different parts of the world, we often fence *out* the common, leaving millions of peasants scrambling for work in urban areas to survive. We must like it that way. It makes people and things and land more "efficient," easier to use up. This historical interlude of abundant resource exploitation provides us with mechanical and technical servants — labor-saving devices that free the rest of us to "specialize" in abstract work such as designing new chemical poisons and food preservatives, programming complex food distribution systems, and financing large agribusiness projects. The field work that peasants do, hoeing the weeds and planting the seeds, has been largely superseded by chemical sprays and giant machines.

My personal heroes are either peasants or those who look at life with a peasant's perspective: organic family farmers and socially oriented small business owners, living and working in the margins and around the edges. I look to large souls with peasant sensibilities — Vincent van Gogh, Leo Tolstoy, Wendell Berry, Dorothy Day,

Mohandas Gandhi, Cesar Chavez, Jesus — when I want to take a personal value check. These are the lives I go to in my own heart to reckon how I'm doing. And I'm always so very far away from their noble examples.

Son of a Preacher Man

As I've said, I'm the son of an Okie preacher, a PK, or preacher's kid, as they used to call us. My father, Orville Smith, who died recently at age ninety, was a fundamentalist, evangelical, Holy Roller, fire and brimstone, Pentecostal, faith-healing, miracle-believing, Assemblies of God preacher. He believed there was only one way to find God, to find truth, and it was his way using his belief system. Any and every other way was "of the devil" and anyone not believing his strict, literal interpretation of scripture would burn in fire and brimstone forever and ever.

"There's this great joke," writes author Anne Lamott, "about a man who dies and goes to heaven and is being shown around by the angels who are saying, 'Over there are the rolling hills where it's balmy and sweet, and over there are the mountains with clouds and rain for people who like to be indoors by the fire, and there's meadows and a huge pond over there,' and it goes on and on. And then there's this walled-off compound and the guy says, 'What's that?' And the angel says, 'Oh, that's where we put the fundamentalists. It's not heaven for them if they think anyone else got in.' I'm a Christian who knows that everyone gets in. In fact, I want to be with the smokers and the Jews because I think they're inherently more interesting."

Interesting stuff has come from Assemblies of God boys who grew up in our religion. Jerry Lee Lewis, cousin of Jimmy Swaggart, grew up in Ferriday, Louisiana, to sing "Great Balls of Fire," and Elvis Presley learned how to "shake that thing" during Holy Roller Sunday night church services in Tupelo, Mississippi.

As teenagers in the 1930s, my dad and his brother, Harold,

escaped dust bowl, Depression-ridden Oklahoma and joined thousands of teenagers, hoboes, and bindle stiffs adrift in a world of no
crops and no work, riding the rails, stopping wherever to ask for odd
jobs and food, and looking for a better life — somewhere, anywhere.
Orville and Harold Smith had seen their father standing in his field
weeping at the burnt stubs of corn that he had planted only weeks
earlier on the family farm. Their family's other business, a small
store, bar, and pool hall in Sapulpa, was suffering from the economic
effects of the Depression. They faced the wrenching decision of
leaving home to find their own way. Instead of the traditional rite
of passage after finishing school — to follow their hearts to careers
and families from safe havens of support — they were forced to
wander in hunger and fear as migrants. Often they would be chased
from a town, chased off the boxcars, chased out of wooded camps,
kept on the move, pushed out of people's compassion, perhaps
because there were too many of them to be compassionate about.

The thousands of footloose, disaffected youth were worrisome
for political reasons. A movement had been formed in Germany
among unemployed youth attracted to the message of Adolf Hitler,
with these young men eventually forming the feared Nazi "Brown-
shirts." Thus, within weeks of Franklin Roosevelt's inaugural, he
proposed and created the Civilian Conservation Corps (CCC) as
part of his New Deal, and so Orville and Harold were able to earn
money to send home by building railroads and planting trees. The
CCC employed 2.5 million young men over ten years and probably
saved the country from a revolution. My dad and uncle continued to
hop freight trains and grimly hang atop boxcars until they eventually
found their way to California, and there they found work in the fields
and orchards.

Meanwhile, a few hundred miles away from Oklahoma's bowl of
dust, in Arizona's north Gila Valley near Yuma, another family who
owned a farm, store, and pool hall was also being deeply affected by
the Depression and drought. Forced to sell their home and what

were once thriving businesses, Librado and Juana Chavez and their family moved back to the farm near where Librado had grown up, and where his deeply religious and widowed mother still lived. Sons Cesar and Richard were only dimly aware of the family's changed circumstances, as they were able to get by and eat well off their farm. Saint Eduvigis, the saint who provides home and food to families that don't have them, was Juana's patron saint. She would routinely send her sons out to find a hungry hobo, most often white, who was passing through on his way to California, and bring him in for a simple hot meal. But the Chavezes, too, lost their crops to the spreading drought, lost their farm, and soon joined the migrant workers on their way to California to compete with the Okies for work in the fields and orchards.

Cesar and Richard finished growing up on the road, taking odd jobs when possible, like sweeping the local theater, where they could also watch their favorite Western series, *The Lone Ranger*. As California farms consolidated, grew in size, and became corporate rather than family farms, farm owners moved elsewhere. The living conditions of the Okies and Chicanos working the fields were more easily ignored — out of sight, out of mind — and as more and more landless workers arrived to compete for jobs, pay plummeted, and strikes escalated. John Steinbeck famously brought the nation's attention to the sorrows and destitution of migrant farm labor.

As the country left the Depression behind and went to war, Cesar Chavez would eventually join and serve in the U.S. Navy, return to civilian life, get married, become involved in registering voters and working for civil rights in community organizations, and then establish the United Farm Workers Union with his wife, Helen, and Dolores Huerta. In 1968, I joined their efforts.

Meanwhile, my dad found a steady job in Sacramento, found religion, started a family, graduated as a minister from a Bible school in San Francisco, and then loaded his young family into his Buick Roadmaster, with an Airstream Silverliner trailer hooked to the back, to begin preaching his way across the United States. For a year, he worked as an evangelist, saving souls for Christ. We ended up broke on the Tamiami Trail near Miami, Florida, with my dad fishing in the canal for our supper. After pastoring a church in Miami for a while, he attracted enough supporters to break off and form his own congregation and build his own church.

Tent Revivals

One of my dad's contemporaries was Oral Roberts, who got his start as a traveling faith healer with a tent. The first time he visited Miami, Roberts pitched his tent in a vacant lot next to my dad's church. There were many others like him traveling around the South in the fifties, men like A. A. Allen and Jack Coe. You can look them up today on the Internet and get a sense of what a tent revival, sometimes called a crusade, was all about.

These guys had once traveled around doing weeklong revivals in churches, but soon churches were not large enough to pack in the crowds and bring in the big bucks. So they moved up to big tents that seated the thousands they would attract. Soon, the most dynamic and charismatic preachers began competing to claim the biggest tent, leapfrogging ahead of each other with the latest, greatest, biggest tents. It wouldn't be long, however, before television began to dominate the evangelistic circuit. The evangelists folded up their tents, and the most dynamic and photogenic of them built TV studios and began bringing in the *really, really big* bucks.

Let me set the scene of a tent crusade for you: Several weeks before the revival, the evangelist announces that he is coming to town. In the supporting churches, excitement begins to build. A "movement of the Holy Spirit begins to flow like a mighty wind." A "mighty work" is about to take place. Masses of sinners are going to come forward and be saved. Hundreds of the sick are going to be healed.

Then, several days before the revival is to begin, tractor-trailer rigs, painted with the evangelist's image and promises that "Jesus

Saves and Heals," and loaded down with canvas and poles and chairs and lights, rumble down Main Street and pull onto a large empty lot. Several dump trucks arrive and scatter loads of pine shavings and sawdust. A massive construction of canvas is unloaded and stretched over the sawdust while poles and lights are strategically placed around the circumference.

Once the tent has been pulled taut and secured from all directions, the lights are strung and tested. A large platform is built under one side of the tent, and thousands of chairs are set up facing it. Now the crucial ramp is built in front of the platform. This will accommodate the throngs of people who will come on crutches and in wheelchairs to receive the prayers and anointing of the evangelist. In front of the ramp, thick-armed carpenters construct a long altar for those who will nightly move forward to kneel in the sawdust to surrender and pray, to accept salvation and be born again.

From one truck come wheelbarrows filled with the abandoned crutches from past crusades. These will be strung around the platform, attesting to the many past healings of this particular evangelist. Like the CEO who proclaims his standing by owning the sleekest, most expensive company jet, success for evangelists is determined by the size of the tent, the number of center poles, and how many abandoned crutches are displayed on the platform.

One cannot help but admire this carefully staged spectacle and its understanding of crowd psychology. Each night, ambulances will arrive with the sick from surrounding hospitals, and the bedridden will be lined up behind the platform for the evangelist to pray over. The service begins with hymns and the performances of talented musicians. People don't come just to watch, but to participate. They will babble, shout, and swoon; they will dance in the aisles, run around the perimeter laughing their heads off, and drop and roll around in the sawdust. Their emotions will be raised to a fevered pitch, then lowered, then raised again repeatedly. This contagious outpouring and emotional release, supported by a community of like-minded believers, is crucial to the sick who have come to experience their healing, and to the sinners who want to reform their ways, cleanse their souls, and leave reborn into a new life, embraced once again by a religious community sharing their faith in God. The evangelist's constant refrain will be: "By your faith in Jesus you are healed." Miracles did seem to happen, with the lame tossing away their crutches and walking freely, but it was hard to verify the more amazing claims. My dad once spent part of our summer vacation trying to track down a guy Oral Roberts asserted had been healed. Roberts said in his newsletter that the man had suffered a partial amputation of his arm. After Roberts prayed over him, the arm was now growing back. Dad couldn't find him.

To get any attention in a business culture of promotion, advertising, and entertainment, a religion that depends on proselytizing and evangelism must also learn the rules of business. Building a church and a congregation is much like building a business and a customer base. I learned a lot about this from my dad and his work.

First Branding Lesson

After preaching around Miami, my dad was asked to pastor the Second Assembly of God Church there. The first thing he did was change the church name. He reasoned, "If we're the second church, wouldn't people rather attend the first?" He changed the name to Central Assembly of God and thus taught me my first business lesson: Never associate your brand name with being second-best.

First Advertising Lesson

Dad mounted two four-foot-high flashing neon signs, one on either side of his church. On one side it flashed, over and over: "Jesus Is Coming Be Ready...Jesus Is Coming Be Ready." On the other: "Prepare to Meet Thy God...Prepare to Meet Thy God."

Dad mellowed some in later years, but he was an intolerant bigot back then. In his heyday, he preached that any "nonbeliever" —

meaning a Jew, Catholic, or member of any religion that did not accept his fundamentalist belief system — would surely burn in hell. That's pretty severe punishment for having a simple difference of opinion.

But of course, Dad *did not* put ads in the paper that said: "Come to our church or else you're totally screwed forever and ever!" No. In two slogans of just five words each — "Jesus Is Coming Be Ready," and "Prepare to Meet Thy God" — were contained some of the most effective and efficient ad copy ever written. He accomplished it all: (1) he described the product, (2) communicated the benefit, (3) warned about the competition, (4) asked for the order, and (5) urged a quick decision.

First Customer Service Lesson

Fundamentalists like the ones I grew up with tend to emphasize the Old Testament God, a "jealous and fearful God" who seems to frown a lot and get really pissed off at the people he created, covering them in boils and turning them into salt statues. On the New Testament side, fundamentalists also emphasize the negative, with heavy doses of agony and suffering forever in hellfire. Nevertheless, as a kid I really liked Jesus because he wasn't nearly as cantankerous as his father and he said some really great things, like: "Do unto others as you would have them do unto you." That lesson wasn't lost on me. Even years later as I moved into business, I recognized this was also the first rule of good customer service. It is much, much better than the Old Testament "eye for an eye and tooth for a tooth," which tends to reduce business prospects, certainly for optometrists and dentists.

Fool's Gold

Faith in God, which has held communities together and produced incredible generosity toward those in need, is sometimes manipulated by those seeking riches for themselves. Oral Roberts has preached the "give-to-get" doctrine of "Seed Faith" for many years, and variations of it have made many other televangelist ministers rich. It goes something like this: By giving your 10 percent "tithe" and more to God, by giving money to the preacher even if you cannot afford it, you are planting a seed that will then grow and come back to you in the very near future after increasing manyfold. You will be blessed with prosperity. The increased amount will not come back from the church or the preacher you gave it to, but rather it will mysteriously appear from God through some unforeseen miracle. If it doesn't come back, then you just didn't have enough faith, or you didn't give generously enough, and you need to "get your heart right with God." But that's still okay, because however strong your faith, your giving will be rewarded in Heaven, providing an eternal rate of return.

This is a corruption of the natural, spiritual truth that faith is rewarded by action, that by working with nature, investing time and energy planting and nurturing seeds, we can produce an abundance of food, just as investing time and energy and money nurturing our community will produce a future abundance of commonwealth, care, and love. Rather than encouraging us to give to the poor in our community who need help with real, basic, survival needs, the Seed Faith notion manipulates our faith to make a rich preacher wealthier now, while we wait for our own returns in the sweet by-and-by. Rather than nurturing faith in ourselves and in each other to help in times of need by giving and investing our income in our local communities and neighborhoods, we are asked to play a rigged scheme of faith lotto.

In his book *God's Politics*, evangelical minister and community organizer Jim Wallis, who lives in inner-city Washington, D.C., says something very different about what the future holds for applied faith:

> *"Faith will be defined more by action than by doctrine. The great moral issue will become poor people. More and more people will ask why we're*

spending more for cosmetics, pet food, and ice cream than on making a decent and dignified life possible for the world's poorest people. Diverse religions and spiritual traditions will learn to live together. The enormous and growing gap between the rich and the rest of us is a real problem for democracy and religion. Wal-Mart will sell us everything unless we act strategically as consumers to restore a genuinely free and diverse market-place and as citizens support a revitalized labor movement. More and more affluent families will get off the pressure train and adopt simpler lifestyles. Hope will be the most essential ingredient for social change."

Faith Based

At ten years of age I became ill with what turned out to be pneumonia and was sick in bed for several days. My dad, a faith healer, brought in members of the church to help him pray for my recovery, but I continued to worsen. As my lungs clogged up and my breathing became more labored, my dad's ministry was on the line. After all, according to the Bible, Abraham was willing to sacrifice his son to God, and God had sacrificed his son, Jesus, so why shouldn't Orville be asked to do the same? A doctor could not be called because that would betray his faith. I worsened further and began struggling for breath in a darkened room. The prayers continued. I realized that their faith was about to get me dead. I yelled out, "Call an ambulance, I need oxygen!" That broke the spell. I was rushed to the hospital and survived. My dad's ministry also survived, but with a more realistic openness to other alternatives when prayers and faith are not enough. A doctor saved me.

When I was four years old, we were driving across the Golden Gate Bridge one day in a four-door sedan. I was in the back seat horsing around with another kid. In those days of no seat belts, the handles that opened the doors pushed down, and the back doors opened from the front, rather than the back, making them vulnerable to swinging open violently in the wind if opened while moving. I fell against the door handle, opening the back door, and went out headfirst toward the rushing pavement. I can still see the front tire of the car in the next lane under which I was headed. My dad, sitting in the right front seat, heard the door open and without time to turn and look, instinctively reached back and grabbed me by my left foot, yanking me back from certain doom. My dad saved me.

What does faith mean to you? For me, faith is first a confidence in ourselves and in each other that grows as our mutual trust is demonstrated. Faith is also a confidence in truth and values, especially in our own personal truth and values as we go within and make the effort to identify them for ourselves in our own situations.

To start any new business, one must have a great deal of faith and confidence just by taking responsibility for it. That responsibility includes those we will be working with, others we will be serving, and the greater community. Responsibility requires empathy, caring, and fairness. The old, outdated model of strict, hierarchical, top-down authoritarianism is no longer a viable way of structuring business in a world of democratic, wide-open communications and information that allows everyone into the game. Some argue that strict hierarchical authority is the only way to control a massive, transnational business, but the policies, corruption, and emotionally sterile, bare-fisted competition that are also said to be necessary have created a work culture without human feeling and spiritual meaning. And there are successful, large company models based on participatory democracy that put to shame the rigid structures that currently rule and ruin so many potentially creative lives. I'll describe some of these in chapter 5.

Some people who start and run businesses have faith only in themselves, or in a small inner circle, distrusting all others. They believe that they can heroically overcome all odds single-handedly, that they and only they know best, and that no one else really matters. They believe that any one cog in the machine is easily and quickly replaceable and has no rights other than to be paid for their work, and that should be as little as possible. They believe that "the

Golden Rule means, he with the gold rules." This is played out financially by CEOs who are now averaging three hundred times what the
average wage earner in their company makes, and it is played out
nationally by the politically motivated widening gap between the
rich and the poor.

Research tells a different story. Bestselling business books by
well-respected business guru Jim Collins demonstrate that companies led by modest, unassuming, caring leaders are more successful
financially than those run by charismatic superstar action heroes.
Research by Diane Swanson, associate professor of management at
Kansas State University, shows that the executives who downplay
ethics and values in their decision making are also the ones who
demand extraordinarily high salaries for themselves, while executives who consider ethics and values in their decisions prefer more
fair pay throughout their organizations. She also shows that the less
values-oriented executives had received more business education —
evidence that modern business education teaches greed and self-
centeredness instead of service to the community.

The business leaders of the future, usually found now in smaller
businesses, have a more realistic, modest sense of themselves, understanding that any successful company, large or small, is successful
because its leaders have put their faith and trust in a great many other
people who are also responsible for the overall success of their company. They respect others as people, not chess pieces. They have
faith in the innate goodness and work ethic of others, and as a result,
they find this faith to be well founded. They understand human
behavior and are patient in allowing the evolution of good values to
succeed. They have studied the wisdom traditions, or have adopted
a spiritual practice for inner guidance and openness to others in their
decision making, or simply had good parenting and a broad education. They treat others as they would like to be treated. They do not
dominate their companies and employees but work with them. They
are minimally hierarchical, sharing ownership and decision making

with employees, and though they themselves might not make as much money as they would otherwise, they understand that sharing and cooperation will create a more successful business that rewards more people, more justly and honorably, and that there are greater personal rewards in worthwhile work than mere money can provide.

Meaningful work comes alive
with faith in others as well as ourselves.
And that requires hope....

CHAPTER TWO

hope

[soul school]

Truth is within ourselves; it takes no rise
From outward things, whate'er you may believe.
There is an inmost center in us all,
Where truth abides in fullness; and around,
Wall up wall, the gross flesh hems it in,
This perfect, clear perception — which is truth.
A baffling and perverting carnal mesh
Binds it, and makes all error; and to KNOW
Rather consists in opening out a way
Whence the imprisoned splendor may escape,
Than in effecting entry for a light
Supposed to be without.

— Robert Browning, "Paracelsus," part 1

Death is not the greatest loss of life. The greatest loss is what dies inside us while we live.

— Norman Cousins

The one thing in the world of value is the active soul.

— Norman O. Brown

Dark Nights of the Soul

I wonder if you've ever lost hope? I once was not able to get out of bed much for several weeks; I just could not get up. I feigned ill health, but it was a deep emptiness and vague fear that left me weak, helpless, hopeless, useless. I was working in computer systems at a distribution center for a foreign car company. They were planning a move to another location a couple of hours away, and there wasn't much for our department to do until the move was made. We spent our time doing little projects to keep busy, and we would take long lunches playing hearts and joking around. As boring as the time was, it was a secure, well-paid job with lots of benefits. When it came time to make the move and I was faced with relocating, I knew that if I stayed with the company, this would be my life from then on. Safe, secure, well paid, unfulfilling, boring. I quit and went to bed.

Several weeks of intense spiritual searching and reading in philosophy and religion ensued. I was bogged down with what a mess the world was in and what a mess I was in. Malcolm X had been assassinated, Watts had exploded in riots, antiwar protests were escalating, and the My Lai massacre in Vietnam had just been exposed (more on that later). So much was wrong, yet I felt I was not contributing meaningfully. I remember reading an Eastern guru and finding him to be profoundly intelligent, creatively engaging, and completely unintelligible. Everything I had ever believed was being brought into question, and for the life of me, I could not understand what the man was saying. It left me with nothing, and I sank deeper into depression.

Of course, that was what the guru was trying to do. Like a modern Buddha, he was calling into question every belief about religion, the values of our culture and society, the foundation of my personal psychological security system, and what I was doing in my life and work. And he left nothing whatever to replace it with, leaving it all up to me. For a while, I lost the will to live.

Sometimes drastic transitions from one way of life to another demand the complete falling away of all support systems. You may not even know what is going on inside you except that you feel like shit. Our minds can break down when we find ourselves without meaning and purpose.

Internationally renowned psychiatrist Viktor Frankl, who endured years of unspeakable horror in Nazi death camps, wrote this in his groundbreaking book *Man's Search for Meaning*:

> *I published a study devoted to a specific type of depression I had diag-nosed in cases of young patients suffering from what I called "unemploy-ment neurosis." And I could show that this neurosis really originated in a twofold erroneous identification: being jobless was equated with being useless, and being useless was equated with having a meaningless life. Consequently, whenever I succeeded in persuading the patients to volun-teer in youth organizations, adult education, public libraries, and the like — in other words, as soon as they could fill their abundant free time with some sort of unpaid but meaningful activity — their depression disap-peared although their economic situation had not changed and their hunger was the same.*

Frankl developed "logotherapy." *Logos* is a Greek word that denotes "meaning," and his therapy was based on the "striving to find a meaning in one's life," which he felt was "the primary motivational force in man." What matters is "not the meaning of life in general, but rather the specific meaning of a person's life at a given moment.... Everyone has his own specific vocation or mission in life to carry out a concrete assignment which demands fulfillment. Therein he cannot be replaced, nor can his life be repeated. Thus, everyone's task is as unique as is his specific opportunity to implement it."

And that is why I'm writing this book to you right now, and why you are reading it right now. "The more one forgets himself — by giv-ing himself to a cause to serve or another person to love — the more human he is and the more he actualizes himself... self-actualization is possible only as a side-effect of self-transcendence."

Wilson Van Dusen, a clinical psychologist, philosopher, and author, echoes Frankl's observations. As a doctor of clinical psychology, he worked for many years at a mental hospital with the most serious cases of mental illness. He defines madness as "a turning in on one's self that makes one a constricted uselessness that misses one's highest potential . . . mad people are relatively useless both to themselves and to others. . . . Usefulness and acting constructively toward others is therefore the way out of madness." He discovered that trying to analyze people out of their madness by attempting to rearrange their inner mind simply didn't work, and that the treatment that brought inner change was accomplished by having the patient perform small, useful chores. As the patient begins feeling useful again, the inner becomes rearranged by the actions of the outer. "The inner is, after all, a symbolic commentary on the relationship of the person to the world. . . . The reality of the inner is in what a person does. . . . Sanity is usefulness."

What if you find yourself in a job with a useless company that makes useless or even harmful stuff, engaged in daily work that is beneath your potential, and beneath your own value system? You're part of a company that's basically gone bonkers. You can't really analyze your way out because you end up simply justifying your situation, but you want to make your way to your real purpose. You can't just leave because that would be irresponsible to others who depend on you for support. Following Frankl's and Van Dusen's advice, your first step might be to find something that is of real service, like volunteering for a local aid organization. As your inner self responds and changes, you are back on the journey of finding your true purpose, which is to match up what you are best at giving with what the community truly needs.

I've heard mythologist Joseph Campbell's advice misstated as "Follow your bliss and the money will come." That's not what he said. He actually said: "If you follow your bliss, you will always have your bliss, money or not. If you follow money, you may lose it, and you will have nothing." He advised taking a first step toward the gods, whereby "they will then take ten steps toward you." That first step brings the psychological support needed. Then, as you progress, your true vocation comes into focus and your choices come from knowing rather than guessing.

Eventually I got back in touch with my surroundings and climbed back out of the hole. I sold my Porsche, lived on my savings for a while, and eventually found the most life-changing work I've ever experienced. I feel lucky. Some never return from depression. It was then that I recognized how short our precious lives are, how quickly they can disappear.

Soul School

Guy Murchie wrote a wonderful book called *The Seven Mysteries of Life*, published in 1978 and still in print. Subtitled *An Exploration in Science and Philosophy* and almost 700 pages in length, it was called by one reviewer "a staggering work of encyclopedic proportions, with a stirring noble vision to match." Murchie's artful combination of scientific explanation and visionary, mystical spirit is both challenging and inspirational.

Murchie writes, "The only hypothesis for the nature of this troubled world that fits all the known facts [is] the hypothesis that planet Earth, is, in essence, a Soul School." He asks us to test that hypothesis by imagining that we are God, intent upon creating a world for the creatures we are creating to live in. Could we "possibly dream up a more educational, contrasty, thrilling, beautiful, tantalizing world than Earth to develop spirit in?" Would we want to make the world comfortable, safe, and free of danger, or "provocative, dangerous, and exciting" — as it is? He then goes on to say that the tests we meet in life are not to punish us but are here to "reveal the soul to itself," that the world is a "workshop...for molding and refining character."

Whether you interpret this as allegorically or literally true, Soul School is where mystery, psychology, and spirituality meet. We slowly but surely learn the lessons of wisdom if we are seeking them, or we ignore them at the peril of our own character and life purpose. Our failings have consequences, to ourselves and to others, that are not magically undone through a belief system. As we sow, so do we reap. That is the moral order that we learn as adults to take responsibility for. It is what traditional wisdom and most religions teach.

Seeing life as Soul School can also show us how we find meaningful work. Through the knocks and challenges of life, we find out who we are, what we really care about. Each time we pick ourselves back up and start again, we draw closer to our meaning. If we take the scary leaps that are sometimes necessary to do what we are here to do, or to figure out what needs doing that best fits who we are, we are on the mythical hero's path to find the work that has meaning for us. "We must be willing to get rid of the life we've planned," Joseph Campbell said, "so as to have the life that is waiting for us.... [E]very process involves breaking something up. The earth must be broken to bring forth life. If the seed does not die, there is no plant."

Whole Earth Heroes

It was on the pages of the *Whole Earth Catalog*, beginning in the late sixties, that I and many others first encountered new, alternative ideas about Gaia, whole systems, the conservation of resources, ecoethics, organic and biodynamic gardening and farming, permaculture, well-made tools, solar and owner-built homes, domes, organic food by mail, soy foods, voluntary simplicity, and foraging. New, different heroes began emerging in our consciousness.

Stewart Brand, creator of the *Whole Earth Catalog*, called *Walden*, Thoreau's book about living simply, "the prime document of America's third revolution, now under way." But, of course, in our culture you can't live simply unless you've got lots and lots of really good stuff. We didn't want to be materialists like our parents, so we called all our stuff "tools," which made them okay.

In Brand's catalog, we met some unique and interesting people with new ways of living and looking at the world, and we learned some disturbing information. We learned about going back to the land and living self-sufficiently. We learned that pesticides and pollution were potentially the death of nature (the United States now applies twice the amount of pesticides as in 1962 when Rachel Carson published *Silent Spring*, which sounded the alarm about poisonous chemicals and helped launch the environmental movement). We learned that we were devastating the planet and that there were smart solutions that were being ignored. We learned that there were well-proven alternatives to the use of chemicals to grow food. We learned that we don't need meat to get enough protein, and that there is more than enough food in the world to go around; we learned that hunger is caused by a scarcity of democracy, not food. We learned that nuclear war would murder nature, creating a nuclear winter that would result in the total loss of human agricultural and societal support systems, and eventually all humans on Earth.

Here, in the pages of Brand's catalog, our whole way of life and our value system were being brought into serious question, and here creative solutions were also being presented. And the encyclopedic diversity of opinions, questions, and answers felt like a whole new world and hopeful way of living being born before our eyes.

Seeking

The gulf between *what was* and *what could be* heightened tensions in the culture. When fundamental questions are being raised and the old answers are no longer believable, that first question mark you allow into your own consciousness can doom your comfy little belief system. The world you never questioned — because "that's just the way it is" and "here are the answers given in the Holy Book" and "comments like that are blasphemy and will get you eternal damnation" — suddenly gets held up for scrutiny. What you see going on around you conflicts with everything you've been told. Values voiced, but not lived. Beliefs stated, but not followed and making no sense. It might start with an unjust war. It might start with discovering a hidden priestly perversion in your church. Then it all comes tumbling down around you, and you're left with the most important and scariest realization you've ever had in your life: They seem so absolutely certain and sure of themselves — these authorities who say they know — but *they don't know*! Just because they say so doesn't make it so.

I'd grown up in church. My identity was firmly attached to a religion that had all the answers. Now, as the tensions of the Civil Rights movement and the escalating war in South Vietnam increased relentlessly, and sides were being taken in politics and the culture, everything was up for questioning.

I remember so well the last fundamentalist church service I attended. The pastor was lamenting all the "lost souls" in foreign lands, and he said everyone in the congregation was to blame. Not only would the heathen go to hell forever and ever if they rejected Jesus as their personal savior, but they would also go to hell because they had never even heard about Jesus, and we were each to blame for not caring enough or giving enough money to send missionaries there to tell them what was going to happen to them and how they could escape. I had heard this so many times before and never thought twice about it. But within the context of the questioning going on inside me, and all around me, I began understanding the implications for the first time.

Wait just a minute, I thought. No way! That couldn't be the truth! If God was a God of love, he wouldn't create people who'd never heard of Jesus and then condemn them to be burned forever because others failed to tell them. I was born with a brain as well as a heart, and that sermon, and the whole belief system behind it, suddenly became unacceptable. The Bible commands that we are to love God with all our mind, heart, and soul, but this was stupendously cruel. If we, the lucky ones, were then to go to heaven, how could we selfishly enjoy it knowing what our friends "down below" were going through?

The dots magically disconnected, and I was pissed! Up I stood and out I walked, leaving behind my safe little life. I needed better answers than that. I was totally uninterested in living forever with the tyrannical, vindictive, monstrous God being offered by my religion. Why didn't he follow his own Golden Rule? What kind of faith and hope was that? I'd take my chances elsewhere.

But church was my identity. Church was my community. I was lost. Where was some truth I could count on, truth that spoke to my heart, that registered in my brain, that made some sense?

"Why should not we also enjoy an original relation to the universe?" Emerson asked. "Why should not we have...a religion by revelation to us, and not the history of theirs?"

Friends Meeting

While the Vietnam War was still in its infancy, two little old ladies arrived at the Stanford Shopping Center in Palo Alto, California, every Saturday morning at 11:00 and stood silently at the entrance for an hour protesting the war. They were there every Saturday without fail, and they were alone in their protest for months. But as the war became an issue in the press, others began joining them, and in 1968, the year Martin Luther King Jr. and Robert Kennedy were assassinated and the Tet offensive in South Vietnam exposed the futility of the war, hundreds stood with them in protest. Those faithful, steadfast, responsible, unintimidated little old ladies were "bearing witness" to their beliefs, and their efforts were gathering momentum.

As I walked through the crowd to do some shopping, I stopped and asked them who they were. They told me they were Quakers, members of the local Religious Society of Friends. Out of curiosity, I visited their church. They met each Sunday for "Friends Meeting" in their plain, no-frills meetinghouse, with twenty or thirty chairs on each side facing each other. People quietly filed in, the doors were closed, and there was silence. Some sat with eyes open, others with eyes closed. Some seemed to meditate, others to contemplate, others to pray. This went on for some thirty or forty minutes of increasing uneasiness on my part, when finally an older woman got to her feet and began relating how a book she was reading had challenged her and what it meant in this time of war and social upheaval.

What blew me away, because it was outside the realm of my own experience, was that the book this older, grandmotherly woman talked about was by Hermann Hesse, an author then popular with young people that was also in my stack of bedside reading. These Quakers were people, young and old, who were questioning and examining their values. After she sat down, another two or three people rose and reverently said a few words of faith, inspiration, or insight, or quoted scripture. Then there was quiet again before everyone stirred, joining hands all around for a few more minutes of silence. Then, with a hand squeeze passed from one to the other, the meeting was over. No pastor, no sermon, no choir, no organ, no hymnals, no stained glass, no doctrine, no creed, no dogma, and no one in charge. Any "authority" came from within themselves. I was moved and forever changed.

Quakers believe that there is "that of God in everyone," the "inner light." They believe we can have a direct experience of God and therefore we don't need any middlemen to mediate between us and Spirit. They combine mysticism (seeking within) and activism (applying values). Even though their religion is rooted in Christianity, they don't accept the idea of original sin or believe in a God who whimsically rewards and punishes. There was no "fall from grace" because the first woman ate an apple, no need for a redeemer or atonement or plan of salvation. Quakers look for the truth within themselves and within their "Meetings for Worship." By seeing "that of God in everyone," they overcome self-centered individualism. They believe in a life of simplicity, service, and love, and in letting their lives speak for who they are. For them, the Bible is the word of God only as interpreted by each person for themselves. Sacred revelation is not only found in the Bible but continues today. They believe in responding to injustice with peaceful noncooperation rather than either violence or acquiescence. They are pacifists, following the Christian teachings of compassion, not returning evil for evil, and not killing their fellow human beings. In their 1660 statement to King Charles II of England they wrote: "We utterly deny all outward wars and strife and fighting with outward weapons for any end or under any pretence whatsoever, this is our testimony to the whole world." During the Vietnam War, many conscientious objectors and antiwar activists were Quakers.

They believe in walking their talk; they believe that their values apply to what they do every day of their lives. They believe in equality and were involved heavily in the women's suffrage movement — Susan B. Anthony and Lucretia Mott were Friends — as well as the antislavery movement, and the Underground Railroad. And they are strong supporters of the United Farm Workers Union. They may be kind and gentle, but they are definitely not meek and mild. Among Christian communities, Quakers may be the closest of any to practicing the values of fairness and justice that Jesus taught.

And when it comes to meaningful work, their business decision-making process, a version of consensus democracy, is a revelation. The Quaker "Meeting for Business" is based on a reverential "spiritual discernment," a search together for truth, as a group, rather than a pushing of personal desires or agendas. Respect for everyone's point of view, with periods of silence between points offered, and a sober, serious attitude mark the Quaker way of doing church business. It's profoundly moving when first experienced.

The Quaker history of lived values, now extending over hundreds of years, gives us hope that fairness and justice will continue to progress despite the huge steps backward that occasionally occur. Ridicule from those protecting the status quo has failed to extinguish the Quakers' inner light, an insistent beacon of truth and equality for the rest of our culture. There's no better illustration of their commitment than their treatment of women. Many churches still teach that God created women as inferior beings and that women must always obediently submit to their husbands. But the Quakers, way back in the 1700s, had already progressed into the twentieth century, voluntarily relinquishing the privileged positions of men. They recognized that women were not participating fully in their Meetings for Business, as most women would not "nay-say" their husbands. So they decided to form two separate "Meetings for Business." They built their meetinghouses with a movable divider down the middle. During Meetings for Worship, the divider was raised, but for business meetings the divider was lowered, creating two rooms so each gender could run separate business meetings. If they needed a common agreement, each group would send an emissary to the other meeting. They continued this practice until there was no longer a concern over whether women would feel free to disagree with their husbands. Their patience and commitment of time to make things fair and just, and to reach agreement, is a commendable and prudent devotion to the most basic democratic values.

As businesspersons in the 1600s, the Quakers' integrity and honest dealing would not allow them to haggle over prices, as was the common practice of their day. Instead, they believed that it was dishonest and deceitful to ask a higher price than what they would accept. Their prices were thus set and nonnegotiable. According to *A Quaker Book of Wisdom*, written recently by Robert Lawrence Smith, a practicing Quaker:

> *Early in the history of the labor movement, Quaker businessmen recognized that unions were essential as a means of communication between management and workers. Many saw collective bargaining at its best as similar to the search for consensus that goes on at Quaker Meetings for Business. Viewed this way, negotiations become a method for bringing about an enlightened resolution or synthesis of different points of view.*

One result is that, by and large, workers at Quaker businesses have been able to reach fair contract terms without resorting to strikes.... The fact is, many Quaker businesses have demonstrated that profit and social responsibility are not only compatible, but interdependent. Big business enterprises today have become increasingly bottom-line oriented. Rather than being accountable to their customers, they are accountable only to their stockholders. They demonstrate their success not by the public regard they've engendered but by pointing to the figures at the bottom of the profit/loss balance sheet. The Quaker business model seeks coopera-tion, while recognizing the need to compete. Instead of seeing their work-ers and customers as adversaries, they view them as partners. Quaker businesspeople understand that they are accountable to the individuals they employ, the customers they serve, the community they share, and their own conscience. Not surprisingly, this adds up to both good citizen-ship and good business.

This unassuming and gentle Quaker meetinghouse in Palo Alto became my center of comfort and community while I transitioned to a new way of understanding and found a new place in the world. I look back with deep regard and respect to the way of the Friends. They saved me.

What Would Leo Do?

The Quakers show us that the practice of loving-kindness summa-rized by the Golden Rule has practical application in our social and political systems. Another source of wisdom I discovered during this time, to my surprise, was the great novelist Leo Tolstoy. Although much more socially progressive in his day than was my dad, the nineteenth-century Russian novelist and philosopher saw the world through the same colorless lens, that is, in black and white. He saw no compromise.

Although famous for *War and Peace* and other fiction, Tolstoy later grew weary of the emptiness of his life and social milieu and began studying what he called "true Christianity" — that is, the teachings of Jesus rather than the doctrines and dogmas of the Russian Orthodox Church. His fiction became moralistic, and in widely circulated essays he began taking on the Church, political institutions, art, culture, and everything else he saw as false and meaningless. His writing struck me deeply. This was a successful and intelligent man of the world thinking for himself, approaching the subject both rationally and emotionally, and with the same righteous indignation I was feeling. Basing his beliefs in the teachings of Jesus, rather than church interpretations and creeds, Leo had this to say back in the late 1800s: "The mistake of all political doctrines, from the most conservative to the most advanced, which has brought men to their present pitiful condition, is the same: the belief that it is possible to keep men social by means of violence."

And this: "[L]ove is only love when it is given in the same degree to outsiders, to the adherents of other religions, and even to the enemies who hate us and do us harm.... [T]his means that violence directed against you can never justify the use of violence on your part."

Also this: "We will be free from the evil that is torturing and corrupting the whole world, not by preserving the present regimes, or by suppressing them, or by imposing them by force. But by having recourse to this sole rule: each one of us, without worrying about the result to ourselves or others, must in our own lives observe the supreme law of love condemning every form of violence."

Immensely appealing to my young idealism during that time of internal struggle, these tenets were even more fundamental than fundamentalism, more black and white than the doctrines of my church, but they were enforced with loving-kindness rather than condemnation. Leo took the wishy-washy, contradictory lives that Christians around him seemed to live and, like Jesus, denounced them as hypocritical. During a time of war like the one we were living in then — and now — Leo's position was an uncompromising moral condemnation of the wars we supported. Leo's writings on nonviolence had influenced Mohandas Gandhi, and Gandhi's life, in turn, was inspiring the nonviolent civil rights campaigns of Martin Luther King Jr. and Cesar Chavez.

What I was struggling with back then was this question: Can those of us who were raised as Christians and who then discovered some things about Church history, beliefs, doctrines, and creeds we could not subscribe to still believe in the religion's basic values, along with other spiritual teachings? Can we ferret out the true and good from the questionable and nonsensical? Can we incorporate them into our lives because they are the right things to do, and because that is how we want to be treated, rather than because we fear the consequences of violating a belief system? And can we apply them not only to daily life, but to our daily work as well?

Leo and Mo

About this same time I'd started reading about Mohandas Gandhi and discovered that he had learned about nonviolence from reading Tolstoy. I was fortunate to have heroes like Leo and Mo to challenge and inform my own thinking and changing beliefs. And I was beginning to test these new beliefs and values in my daily decisions and work.

One can live only so long with the contradictions in one's life before something has to give. If you have ideals you wish to live by, and your daily compromises with those ideals cannot be ignored, then either the compromises destroy you, or you abandon your way of life and choose a path that is more consistent with your ideals. I chose to abandon my old way of life for something — anything — that was more consistent with my emerging understanding and beliefs.

National Guard

Prior to all this questioning and soul searching, I had enlisted in the National Guard as a clerk typist. It was one of the military's cush

jobs, but when I arrived at Fort Polk, Louisiana, to begin basic training, my manhood was challenged by a tough sergeant trying to make
a quota. He told me I must be a "candy ass" to sign up as a clerk typist. I said I wasn't. He said I was. I said I wasn't. He said, "Prove it."
So I did something really stupid and told him to sign me up for the
infantry. He must have had a good laugh that night with his fellow
sergeants. I spent the next three months slogging through rain and
mud instead of sitting at a desk.

After basic training, I was sent to Fort Ord in California for
advanced infantry training. While I was marching in sand wearing a
sixty-pound backpack and carrying a heavy mortar in the dark at
three o'clock in the morning, my clerk typist friends were typing
away in the morning, spending the rest of their day at the beach,
meeting girls in Monterey after dinner, turning in for a good night's
sleep, and going home for the weekend. Candy asses!

But I got even. Once my six months of active duty were over, I
still faced a five-and-a-half-year commitment of monthly weekend
drills and two-week annual summer camps. So upon returning to my
home base, I immediately transferred to the National Guard Band
unit in my area. I had played trumpet growing up, and although I
hadn't touched it for a while, they had space for a trumpet player and
I could still manage to finger the right notes at the right time. Within
a few months, as the Vietnam War escalated and the draft intensified,
professional musicians were becoming desperate to get into the
band, but we were full. I had made it just in time.

Our two-week summer camps in the California desert with the
National Guard Band were even better than being a clerk typist.
We got up early to march over to some Officer Wanker's cabin and
wake him with Strauss marching songs. Then, while the tanks
headed out in 120-degree heat to play war games, we tuned up in our
air-conditioned rehearsal hall and practiced. After lunch, we lolled
around the pool all afternoon. The tank teams would soon be fighting
and dying in Vietnam while we practiced our scales and rehearsed our

marches, oblivious to the injustice of class distinctions and the luck of the draw.

What Is War Good For?

A Saigon general casually drawing his pistol, aiming it at the head of a newly captured Viet Cong, and blowing him away. Bodies of women and children strewn along a ditch beside the road. A naked young girl running toward the camera crying in pain, trying to out-run the napalm sticking to her skin, burning up her back. A Buddhist monk in lotus position setting himself on fire in Saigon's public square, calmly sitting there as the flames engulf and burn until he slowly topples over without a sound. Students at a quiet Midwestern college lying dead after the National Guard shot into their peaceful war protests.

These images broke our hearts. These images stopped the war. And because they stopped the war, you will not see such images — of innocent children being burned and killed and maimed or the caskets and body bags of our own kids — from now on. "It is not in good taste" is what the media tells us now. Seeing those children suffering from napalm made us angry. Hearing about the random killings of innocents got many of us out of our chairs and into the streets. And the callousness of our scientists and the mercilessness of our corporate "defense" industries drove us down those streets, yelling and chanting in protest.

Then there was the My Lai massacre. On March 16, 1968, two platoons of American soldiers entered the village of My Lai and began shooting unarmed civilians and burning down the village. Elderly men, women, children, babies, water buffalo, cows, pigs, and chickens were blown apart by machine guns and grenades. Groups were herded together and murdered. Sixty to seventy were herded into a ditch and mowed down. More than five hundred people were killed within hours. Some women were gang-raped; other villagers tortured and beaten.

After learning about My Lai (and we know now that this was not an isolated incident), seeing the pictures of babies scattered in the ditches where they had been shot to death, I and many others in the country were devastated. For me, serious questioning continued about my upbringing, my religion, the culture I was born into, and my chosen profession in business. What did it mean that God had commanded us not to kill, yet my Christian culture was killing, and the church I grew up in was not taking a stand against it? Why did my church worship Jesus, who said, "Blessed are the peacemakers," and believe in the Bible that said, "Thou shalt not kill," if my dad wasn't even talking about the war in Sunday services? Why did there seem to be such a disconnect between what Jesus is quoted as teaching and what was being practiced by all of us Americans who professed to be Christians?

And what was the connection between business and the war? What was the connection between my company and the war? What was *my* responsibility for the war while I continued to work for a defense contractor? Was I responsible for the end result of my work? As I wrote computer code, pushed the buttons, mounted the tape drives, printed the reports — just doing my functionary job as well as I could — did I need to worry that the company I worked for made the helicopters and the targeting systems for mounted guns and napalm bombs used to kill innocent civilians in a distant land? Was that my personal responsibility if I hadn't personally aimed the rocket and pulled the trigger?

Joan Baez

While with the Quakers, I served as chair of their Peace and Social Action Committee. Classes in nonviolence were offered by the local Free University, which had been set up to teach what wasn't being taught at nearby Stanford University, and I attended them at the home of a local pacifist. Then one evening, an argument erupted over a fine point in nonviolent theory that ended with two of the students on the floor, fighting! I was serious about my new belief system, and was trying hard to live its values. And here were others who professed these same ideals, yet could so easily ignore them when verbally challenged. I had hoped to find less hypocrisy, but here it was again. Did anybody really live their belief system? It reminded me of the poorly edited church bulletin that announced: "The Peacemaking Committee scheduled for today has been cancelled due to a conflict."

The most famous former member of the Palo Alto Friends Meeting was Joan Baez, who had grown up in it but no longer attended. There she had met her "guru," Ira Sandperl, a mischievous self-described "Gandhian scholar" who taught her the history, theories, and practice of nonviolence. As her musical career took off, Joan and Ira founded the Institute for the Study of Non-Violence, also located in Palo Alto, home of Stanford University and its surrounding research centers. Nearby, in Menlo Park, was Kepler's Book Store, owned by Roy Kepler, a local pacifist and peace activist. Ira and Joan's mom, "Joan, Senior," often worked there. As the Vietnam War escalated, the institute attracted several bright peace activists and draft counselors dedicated to nonviolent resistance to the war. I was soon attending classes there and becoming involved in the institute's projects.

The contradiction between my growing dedication to nonviolence through study and action and my membership in the National Guard soon grew too great to ignore, and I applied for Conscientious Objector (CO) status with eighteen months left in my six-year commitment.

The National Guard was puzzled. A conscientious objector from the band? He's got to be nuts! As part of the process, I was psychoanalyzed by an army psychologist, who in his report judged me to have an "extremely well-integrated personality." But they would not change my status, and I protested by no longer attending regular drills. When my six years were up, they simply discharged me honorably, over my objections, and told me to get the hell out and leave them alone.

I was disappointed. My intention had been to set a precedent. Although he supported the Vietnam War and didn't teach peace, my dad had been a CO during World War II because he refused to kill Christians on the other side. With that history, I had felt I could more easily obtain CO status and then help others obtain theirs.

Illegal, immoral wars of aggression and torture, rather than defense, have now become part of America's political way in the world, and if we continue down this path it's only a matter of time before the draft is reinstituted. The Quakers and other peacemakers regularly teach their children the alternatives of peace and nonviolence, documenting everything they are learning and doing, so when the time comes for their children to enter the draft or resist by filing as a conscientious objector, their kids have a genuine, knowledgeable choice, and can back it up with evidence.

Although we were sincere and fiercely committed to nonviolence and antiwar activities at the Institute for Non-Violence, the real war and its real violence were half a world away. Our ideals, philosophizing, and protests were an important alternative to the daily warmongering on the networks, but were they enough to bring real change? Or were we just a bunch of privileged, risk-averse brats assuaging our guilty consciences while others were fighting and dying to preserve our way of life? Was anything real happening with us? I was restless to engage in real sacrifice for making real change, to step wholeheartedly into the fray and make things different. As part of my nonviolent activities with the Institute for Non-Violence, I enlisted in grape boycott organizing for the United Farm Workers Union. When I ran out of personal savings and could no longer support my volunteer activities, I applied to the Farm Workers Union for financial support and soon found myself meeting Cesar Chavez and being enlisted for a new executive position in the union.

Soul Persists

I don't think we can discuss meaningful work without discussing the spiritual. I consider myself a pilgrim without a spiritual or religious axe to grind or system to sell you. Linking up with our fundamental source is a path toward wholeness and enlightenment, and the spiritual, within a religious tradition or not, is reflected in the work we do and how we do it. We have apparently been born with an inner guidance system, most directly accessible through our inner voice, through prayer, through meditation, the symbology of our dreams, and the myths that underlie our culture. All we need do is open ourselves to it and explore the messages that are constantly being offered. This is crucial to finding vocation, purpose, and meaning, because as we understand ourselves, guidance seems to come from everywhere, and life becomes purposeful and magical. And this is the foundation of hope.

We seem to be intuitive mythmakers, which is a way to make truth available to ourselves as we grow in understanding. An eternal conflict is being waged between the light and the dark, between the spiritual and the material, and every human predicament, every historical situation, is a phase of the struggle. "Be kind," said the philosopher Philo of Alexandria, "for everyone you meet is fighting a great battle."

Every situation we face with our work is also part of this ongoing challenge.

"Enlightened management is one way of taking religion seriously, profoundly, deeply, and earnestly," Abraham Maslow wrote.

Of course, for those who define religion just as going to a particular building on Sunday and hearing a particular kind of formula repeated, this is all irrelevant. But for those who define religion . . . in terms of deep concern with the problems of human beings, with the problems of ethics, of the future of man, then this kind of philosophy, translated into the work life, turns out to

be very much like the new style of management and of organization.... And
the qualities of the superior managers have been worked out, i.e., they are
more democratic, more compassionate, more friendly, more helpful, more
loyal...a certain kind of democratic manager makes more profit for the
firm as well as making everybody happier and healthier.

No matter how much you've explored your inner life, you can still ask the questions that are key to finding meaning in your work. What is it that you most love, most care about? What goes on inside your head and your heart as you first awake, as you drive to and from your job? Though the answer springs from the unconscious, it is your companion. It is your love. It is your addiction. It is your quality. It is your meaning. It is your ruler. What we do reflects our inner life. By looking at what we actually spend our time doing, we can know what our inner life is all about. Unless, of course, what you're doing is killing your inner life.

You may be numb from everyday coping with your job or business. There is the constant hammering of responsibility, the juggling of priorities, the competitors trying to eat your niche for lunch — and gradually, imperceptibly, you deaden. Your work doesn't work for you anymore. It doesn't make you alive anymore. In fact, it has become deadly boring. But what to do? Your security is important, and considering all this is risky. You have a mortgage and car payments. But what if you could be more fulfilled doing something completely different?

You notice that you're beginning not to care much about anything but your own family and close friends. There's just too much sadness and tragedy in the world, way too much to do anything about. There is much more you would like to do, but you need a paycheck and the choices for how to get one are few, so you just soldier on, give where you can, help when you can, but it doesn't fulfill that deep desire for meaning.

Deadening your feelings may be your only way to cope, but the problem is, as Helen Keller reminded us, "The best and most beautiful things in the world cannot be seen or touched. They must be felt with the heart." Closing off our hearts to the pain may also close us off to the feelings of awe and beauty, our reasons for being alive.

Why Work?

Years ago my parents owned a weekend home in a community built around a golf course and lake. There were many bored retirees there, living "the good life" — which seemed to consist of a daily schedule of rising late, getting boozed up in the afternoon, going out to dinner, and crashing early, drunk in front of the tube. Was this worth working a lifetime for?

I tried retiring for a while, still many years before retirement age. We moved our family to acreage in redwood country, off the grid. It was great living in nature, with the river, horses, and goats — paradise. But it wasn't long before restlessness set in. I started driving to town a lot and hanging out in bookstores. Then came complete existential boredom. Was this the American dream everyone was talking about: being useless? Maybe I was a workaholic, needing to cover a hole in my soul by escaping through work. But I certainly didn't feel that. The ennui was much more born of a feeling that I still had work to do, that there was something I was here for, a calling — and it was not to just hang out. There was a specific task, as yet unknown, that only I could do, and if I didn't do it, it would not get done.

I tried some short-term business consulting, but at the time that wasn't my gig at all. There was no connection, no feeling, no hands-on, real work, no team, no context, no mission. Each company seemed to exist solely *to* exist. Their missions seemed to be: "Our core competence is to sell as much stuff as possible (it doesn't matter how or what), so that the people at the top can make as much money as possible by paying the people under them as little as possible." We are already stuffed with stuff, and here was some more stuff. Where there is real care, real quality, real commitment to good, creative work and artful design skillfully wrought, that's not stuff; that's beauty, a crucial and useful aspect of meaning. But when it's just more stuff, a bit of a product tweak that's supposed to be a giant leap forward with great fanfare, who needs it? Where's the calling? Where's the sense of greater purpose?

The world of business has become rather cold and heartless and quietly desperate. Over the past thirty years, as corporations have become increasingly devoted to the bottom line, to the exclusion of every other consideration, and jobs have begun moving to the other side of the world, there hasn't been much alarm in the office. The blue-collar workers downstairs were losing their jobs, but that was okay. That was hand labor, easily replaced by automation and cheap labor overseas. We in the office have education and skills. No problem.

But then something dark started skulking around just outside our peripheral vision, waiting, watching. As consumers, we kept up our daily hunt for the cheapest price — the lower the better. It didn't matter where or how it was made — whether it was a car we were buying, sheets for our bed, or food for our kids — cheap was always better. You could get breakfast for only $2.99, and that included eggs and potatoes, three kinds of meat, juice, and coffee. Never mind the chickens squeezed so tightly together their beaks had to be burned off so they wouldn't peck each other to death. We weren't told about that. Price is important. Never mind the pig shit overflowing into our water supply. They didn't put that on TV. Price is important. Never mind the cancers caused by our industrial food system. One person's good deal often means someone else's raw deal. Price is important.

Then they started coming for us in the office. Programmers in India work a lot cheaper. Price is important. Accountants in Burma have the same computers and programs and can do spreadsheets a lot cheaper. Price is important.

An undercurrent of fear seems to be running through life in the office these days. Anyone's job could be gone in a flash. Facing the various other crises that we're becoming aware of is going to take a lot of creativity.

But fear is not conducive to creativity.

How Are We to Live and Work?

People in every time and place have held in common, through their wisdom traditions, some basic beliefs about our lives and work here on Earth. In modern language, they believed (and believe) that the material world we see, hear, touch, taste, and smell is imbued with living spirit that is aware, intentional, and directional — not random, or by chance, or chaotic. They believe that for an individual's life and work to have meaning and purpose, life itself must have meaning and purpose. They believe that with our freedom of consciousness come responsibilities and duties for the well-being of the whole. They believe that life is verb — pattern, process, and action — not noun — thing, subject, and object. They believe that myths and dreams are truths that bypass our rational ego or mind, that communicate to us directly from our underlying connected consciousness and link our individual intelligence to foundational wisdom. Finally, they believe that our ego or mind — the incessant compulsive chatter from past internal programming that distracts our attention from what is real, here, and right now — should be put to use for the greater good rather than being the master of our personal daily lives.

Our rational, linear world of business and work needs the balance of spirit and wonder and respect for the unknown. That is where the art and creativity of business comes from. How do we find this balance? Is there a Business Muse?

Wavebands of Meaning

In 1965, Edward Matchett began an investigation into the nature of the creative mind that was sponsored by the Science Research Council of Great Britain and received the assistance of hundreds across the world. He wrote that creative energy, which engenders creative action, comes to any creator in a kind of relaxed reaching out..., "the potential creator's whole being outstretched ready to receive.... The focus of attention in every moment is totally on the incoming flow of energy, requiring the full cooperation of all of the person's own spirit, mind and body."

Matchett wrote further that anyone "can experience and produce meaning...simply by becoming open, positive, and receptive to the whole universe," but "there cannot be any superstition or some limiting belief-system that blocks the way. It can be done only in trustful simplicity...and comes in response to our humble need of assistance, our expectation of the best, and our commitment to produce work of real worth."

Matchett saw the individual as a kind of receiver who can tune into a "waveband of meaning," something that we can access by "asking for it truly" because it is what we actually are in our deepest self, and that it comes by being true to what lies deepest within us. It continually calls us to be free by letting "everything everywhere be filled with meaning."

A similar perspective is offered by author Brenda Ueland, who felt that the more we use our creative power, the more we have available to use — and that we should use our creative power "because there is nothing that makes people so generous, joyful, lively, bold and compassionate, so indifferent to fighting and the accumulation of objects and money."

Creative work comes in many forms but is best cultivated in an atmosphere of trust and good cheer. The offices I love working in are fun to be in, even when things may not be looking great for sales, or when the new product isn't selling up to plan. A great place to work never takes itself too seriously. Hard, serious, efficient work gets done, but there's always time for a joke, a light moment, a friendly smile, a helpful comment. A lot can be accomplished with trust and good cheer. Offices of good cheer, doing good work, are conducive to the wavebands of meaning that bring epiphanies of true creativity.

Hope

Without hope in the future, we wander, lost and without meaning — and without the energy to make the positive changes necessary for meaning to come alive. Without a vision based on hope, community is lost. When we lose our way, we sometimes need to retrace our steps to the fork in the road that took us the wrong way, and set out along the path not taken, the path that should have been.

A prime example of this sort of path retaken is found in the person of Alan Chadwick. In 1967, a massive buildup of troops in Vietnam occurred, along with the hippie Summer of Love in San Francisco. The culture was in chaos, at war in Vietnam and at war with itself. Big agriculture was destroying family farms and growing bigger, ever bigger. During that year, Chadwick, an artist, violinist, Shakespearean actor, and master gardener, was hired to create a Student Garden Project on the campus of the University of California, Santa Cruz. Working only with hand tools and organic amendments, Chadwick and his student assistants transformed a steep, chaparral-covered hillside into a prolific garden, bursting with flowers, vegetables, and fruit trees. The informal apprenticeships that students served with Chadwick would eventually lead to the development of the current Center for Agroecology and Sustainable Food Systems, where over a thousand apprentices have been formally trained in what he called "the method."

The history of the garden on the UCSC website has this to say about Chadwick's legacy:

Chadwick introduced a unique approach to gardening, which he called the "biodynamic/French intensive" method. Chadwick set to work on the stony soil with a vengeance, using only the Bulldog spade and fork that Smith & Hawken would one day make popular. By 1969 the brushy hillside had been transformed. From thin soil and poison oak had sprung an almost magical garden that ranged from hollyhocks and artemisias to exquisite vegetables and nectarines. Students were taught how to "double dig" beds to loosen the soil to a depth of two spade blades. The Garden's carefully tended beds, enriched with compost, bone meal, leaf mold, and other amendments could produce up to four times the abundance of traditionally managed plots from the same space.

Chadwick didn't just strive for quantity. His upper class upbringing in Edwardian English society had left him with exacting tastes and an appreciation for fine food that he passed on to his young charges. In an era when all supermarket lettuce was iceberg, all potatoes Russet, and apple choices were either red or green, the Garden boasted heirloom varieties of vegetables, fruit and flowers. This was more than two decades before "California cuisine" would make radicchio, purple beans, and fingerling potatoes standard fare on restaurant menus. "It is not much of a stretch to say that Chadwick and those who trained with him were responsible for the interest in distinctive fruit and vegetable varieties that we see today," says Garden Manager Orin Martin.

Rejecting anything synthetic, Chadwick also helped spur the organic gardening and farming movements, with their craftsman-like approach to soil building and plant care. He used organic inputs to enrich the rocky soil and deplored the use of chemical pesticides. He preached composting — "Life unto death and death unto life" — and emphasized the soil's fragility, warning that, "The skin of the Earth must be approached with great sensitivity... it is fragile and must be protected."

Alan's techniques worked wonders on the inhospitable hillside. In a 1969 article, Sunset *magazine called him "one of the most successful organic gardeners the editors have ever met. Mr. Chadwick believes that a healthy plant is not likely to be eaten or overcome by pests and his intensive kind of culture is such that the plants do stay in great health." Sunset's editors marveled at the transformation of marginal land into an abundant garden, reporting that, "At times during the peak of the flower season, the students cut and placed ten thousand blooms a day at the help-yourself kiosk on the main campus road. And last year the gardeners grew, picked and supplied the college cafeterias with tons of tomatoes."*

Beth Benjamin, a freshman in 1967, recalls, "Alan was simply the most fascinating human being on campus for me. Soon nothing else seemed to come into focus but his garden. I was unhappy and doing poorly in my classes, but in the garden I vibrated with the colors and the smells and the stories Alan told us about the plants and his travels and the new skills I was learning. By April, I convinced my counselor that I wanted a leave of absence, and I could finally devote my full time to the world of plants. As an apprentice, I worked from dawn until dark and was filled with his dreams and our common task of bringing the garden into reality, breaking new ground and tending what we had already planted. He had flaming temper tantrums, told tales, gave us dinner parties, fed us from his own bread and ham and cheese, threw dirt clods at us and laughed as he hid behind the compost piles. He taught us the joy of work, the discipline to persevere in order to make a dream come true even when we were hot and tired, and the deliciousness of resting and drinking tea after such monumental labors. . . . I think of Alan almost every day still, thirty years later, and smile with the memories and with gratitude for all he gave me."

Alan went on to establish garden projects in other areas of Northern California and in Virginia. His student apprentices are now scattered throughout the United States and abroad, growing food and flowers and vineyards organically. His was a path once lost to chemical poison companies looking for new markets after World War II, oblivious to the potential devastation of our health that their "miracles" would bring. Master Gardener John Jeavons adopted his methods to help peasants in the developing world feed themselves and become more self-sufficient. And to import the sturdy Bulldog tools from England that Alan, John, and their apprentices required to establish gardens and small farms, I cofounded Smith & Hawken.

*Meaningful work comes alive
when hope engenders positive change.
And that requires justice. . . .*

CHAPTER THREE

justice

[action heroes]

I've observed that people tend to live at one of two extremes in the spectrum of life: those who live on the edge, and those who avoid the edge. Those who live on the edge are hanging out in the most dangerous and unstable places — yet they're also often the most powerful agents of change, because the edge is where change is happening; away from the edge, things are naturally unchanging.

— Thom Hartmann

Action is the antidote to despair.

— Joan Baez

Our lives begin to end the day we become silent about things that matter.

— Martin Luther King, Jr.

Justice from the Barrel of a Gun

I grew up playing cowboys and indians around the neighborhood, and Hopalong Cassidy was the first cowboy action hero I began imitating. Hopalong was an unlikely name for a silver-haired good guy dressed in black who flashed his guns but always captured the bad guys by outsmarting them. That was the modus operandi of the horse opera cowboys back then. The singing cowboys, Roy Rogers and Gene Autry, were easy on the bad guys, bringing them to justice rather than shooting it out. The bad guys cooperated when there was no escape, quickly realizing that they had been outfoxed by the good guys, and were led off, heads hung sheepishly, to the sheriff or judge to face their fate. The power that came out of the barrel of a gun stayed in the gun. It only needed to be wielded from a position of strength and moral superiority, and the bad guys, recognizing they couldn't go up against what was good and right, always backed down.

For me, finding heroes other than the Jesus Christ taught in our church was not that easy. We were severely limited within the fundamentalist worldview that dominated our daily lives. We seldom saw a newspaper, and my family wouldn't dream of allowing a TV in the house. We were not to be tainted by worldly viewpoints or the sinful world's concerns; we were to "come out from among them and be ye separate," as an oft-quoted scripture verse demanded. But the next-door neighbor had a TV that faced the front screen door and thought nothing of my hanging out on the front porch by the hour, eagerly drinking in the images of *Laurel and Hardy*, *The Little Rascals*, and *Superman*.

When I was around eight or nine I got the teaching of faith kind of mixed up with Superman's ability to fly. I figured that if I put on a cape, got up on the roof of the house, and had enough faith, I could fly too. So I really concentrated hard, practicing creative visualization, building my faith up, and then yelled out, "Up, up, and away..." as I stretched out my arms and gave a very little jump. I certainly didn't have enough faith to leap off our one-story house, much less leap tall buildings with a single bound, and instead my first doubts about faith (and Superman) were born. I think that's when I started looking for some solid evidence upon which to base my beliefs.

I eventually adopted the Lone Ranger as my favorite hero. He was more mysterious, with a tragic past and a no-nonsense demeanor. He would never shoot his silver bullets to *kill* a bad guy; he'd never draw first — just faster — and he'd only shoot to knock the gun out of the bad guy's hand. No preemptive strikes for this cowboy.

In comic books and on TV, cowboys were responsible, they had character and values and acted on them. The Lone Ranger would take on the bad guys: bandits robbing stagecoaches, confidence men relieving widows of their savings, rich cattle barons stealing their neighbor's land. I loved him for that.

Before the Lone Ranger, it had been the cowboys *against* the Indians. And here was a man who had partnered up *with* an Indian. A new ideal was being offered, a first hint that maybe Indians weren't all bad after all. From the Lone Ranger and Tonto I learned that values and loyalty were important, that I shared responsibility for others around me, for the community we are in, and that although the risks faced by a TV cowboy were obviously never that great, seeking justice, standing up for what is right, can sometimes be dangerous.

Armageddon Hero

My dad read the Bible constantly, and he especially loved the book of Revelation. After he retired, he memorized the entire thing. I'm not sure which aspect of the "end times" fascinated my dad: Jesus coming back in "clouds of glory," or the righteous rising up to heaven with him, or the evil unbelievers being left behind getting their comeuppance, burning in hell forever and ever. He believed in the literal interpretation of the Bible and preached often that the Antichrist would rise up and Jesus would battle Satan in the Middle East. The identity of the Antichrist in Christian fundamentalist teaching changes from time to time, but for a while when I was growing up, it was Russia "from the North." Later, my dad wrote a book, supported by many scriptures he had researched, claiming that Hitler would reappear as the Antichrist. In the Bible the Antichrist is variously identified as an individual, a political power, and a religious power. I haven't read the recent zillions-selling *Left Behind* series of books about the end times, but I remember well the shouting, sweaty evangelists grasping their soggy handkerchiefs in one hand and their open Bibles in the other, instilling deep fears in the faithful to soften us up, open our wallets, and keep us in line.

The evangelist would describe hell and its horrors in exquisite detail, where sinners and unbelievers that had been left behind would line up, inexorably moving forward toward the "lake of fire," the burning pit of agony. Upon reaching the rim, each would tumble in to burn forever and ever and ever, their cries unheard by the uncaring god who had offered them the chance of salvation that they would now pay the price of having ignored. Up above, the saved would look down, not in sorrow or empathy but in glee at the torment, pointing their fingers and saying, "I told you but you would not listen, and now you have found out that I was right and you were wrong. Burn, baby, burn."

The evangelists used one technique I most feared: They would address one person, amidst the many in the audience, who had sinned that week: "You know who you are, and I'm speaking to you — this may be your last chance to accept salvation." My heart would pound louder and louder, knowing that I was the one — that I would be lost because I had screwed up again. Any day now, the end was coming; believers had been waiting now for over twenty centuries, but Jesus could return at any time to take the believers up with him to heaven, and I would be left without hope because I didn't come forward and accept salvation the only way it was offered: through this church and this faith on this night.

All this, of course, presented only one version of God believed in by one group of professional holy men. And they had a personal stake in my decision. Each soul saved racked up points on their god's scoreboard, which got them a bigger mansion "just over the hilltop," as one of our hymns celebrated. And before everything and everyone else goes to hell, these men would get to come back, seated at the right hand of their god, and rule over the Earth for a thousand years. This is the world's final fate and ultimate horror and the evangelists' just reward for being right: a kingdom ruled by the preachers, complete with the inquisitions, the debasement of women, and the witch-hunting that always accompanies self-righteous followers and enforcers of a cruel god. We've been through this movie before.

Right-wing Christians like my dad believe in ending the separation of church and state and replacing our democracy with a theocracy, ruled by self-appointed interpreters of Old Testament law rather than our Constitution, which requires us *all* to be responsible for our government. This is the Christian literalist preacher's parallel to the Muslim fundamentalist mullah's utopia. Justice would mean "an eye for an eye" and the Ten Commandments. Peace would not be an issue because the war between Christ and the Antichrist is not a symbol of our inner spiritual struggle or a cool video game; it is concrete and inevitable, skies filled with real nuclear weapons and seas filled with real blood. Government regulatory agencies would be abolished since the things they govern, like the environment and transportation and social services, will be no longer relevant in a world about to be destroyed in the end times.

Why care about exacerbating global warming, dropping a few nuclear bombs, or poisoning the Earth with pesticides and nuclear waste if you're going to be swept up to heaven in the Rapture? When you replace the cause-and-effect law of nature's justice with this twisted vision of religious rule, you create an instant exemption from responsibility. If the believers will be whisked away before the consequences come due, then there is no morality, and there is no justice. Anything goes. It will all be forgiven, so don't you worry your pretty little head about it. This is the ultimate irresponsibility that the Christian right would have us adopt, and makes a travesty of the life and teaching of Jesus, who made responsibility for each other his single, most important request.

People of faith have been in the forefront of American social progress made throughout the nineteenth and twentieth centuries. From the abolition of slavery to women's right to vote, the civil rights movement, the farmworkers' boycott, and beyond, the faith community has led the fight for justice and peace. The Christian right would now tarnish that sterling leadership and sacrifice with gross and deliberate debasement and misinterpretation of holy scripture for their own greed and hunger for power. Scriptural literalists of the Christian right are undermined forever by the very person Christians consider the founder of Christian theology, St. Augustine: "That which is known as the Christian religion existed among the ancients, and never did not exist; from the very beginning of the human race until the time when Christ came in the flesh, at which time the *true* religion, which *already* existed, began to be called Christianity." If true religion existed before theology, why then do people fanatically adhere to various versions of religion? Of course we're going to differ. The true religion, the truth that rests in all of our hearts, in everyone, from antiquity to the endless future, is ours to interpret and live and value and love... endlessly individual, endlessly true, endlessly valued, endlessly loved.

It's a relief to remember that ancient wisdom traditions are now more alive and meaningful than ever. As research conclusively shows, the many world religions all come from the same ancient sources of inner wisdom and lived virtues — sources available to us today from the ancients, from each other, and from our own inner resources. These sources teach a God of love, hope, and bounty; a morality based on personal responsibility for our actions and their consequences for ourselves and others; justice and equality here and now for all; compassion for those less fortunate; and love for our neighbors. They also teach that this one life here on Earth is not all there is.

A Liberal Dose of Democracy

Notions of justice inspired by the wisdom traditions still need effective institutions to do the work of making the world a more equitable place. We haven't yet taken the final step in becoming a true democracy that ensures the balance needed for a true equality of power. That step includes economic democracy along with a more participatory political democracy. In the modern, undemocratic corporation, voting is based on "one dollar, one vote" rather than "one person, one vote." Ownership measured in dollars determines control of the institution.

There is an alternative to this model. Some of the institutions that offer the highest form of democracy by including economic democracy along with political democracy are credit unions, consumer cooperatives, and labor unions. Some might consider these dated answers for different, simpler times. My view is different. Consumer cooperatives continue to thrive across the country and are much beloved by their members. Despite repeated attempts by the banking industry to destroy the credit union competition, credit unions also continue to offer local alternatives that keep community money working within the community. Unions had been a countervailing force to MegaMaw power (see chapter 5). But in recent years the sometimes corrupt labor and trade unions have been undermined by many of their jobs being transferred to Southern "right to work" states and out of the country, by laws that limit their organizing effectiveness, and by succumbing to top-down bossism rather than adhering to democratic principles. With the decline of union effectiveness over the past thirty years, real wages have stagnated and income inequality has exploded. The forty-hour workweek, fought for and won by the union movement, is now a distant dream as the average hours worked continue to increase. We are now out of balance and suffering for it.

A *credit union* is a democratic, cooperative financial institution, created, owned, and operated by its members, with one member, one vote. It is a democratic alternative to the undemocratic bank. A *food cooperative* is a democratic consumer institution, created, owned, and operated by its members, with one member, one vote. It provides a democratic alternative to the undemocratic grocery store chain. A *labor union* is a democratic labor institution, created, owned, and operated by its members, with one member, one vote. It provides a balance to the undemocratic corporation. Whenever there is ill health in the services we offer to each other, a liberal dose of economic democracy is the recommended prescription.

Credit card debt with outrageous interest got you down? Huge, privately held, transnational banks located who knows where, owned by who knows who, doing who knows what with your money, and taking unfairly large profits out of your local community are the illness. Creating and joining local democratic credit unions to keep your money flowing through your own neighborhood is the liberal dose of economic democracy that cures it. We — you, me, and our neighbors — own the credit union, we operate it, and we aren't going to screw ourselves.

Hate the way your boss is treating you and your fellow employees, paying you as little as possible, making who knows how much money, living who knows where, doing who knows what? Greed and unfair distribution of income for work performed are the illness. Creating and joining a democratic union of people who do the work is the liberal dose of economic democracy that cures it. We then have a say in how things are done at the company, and we have leverage for a more equitable distribution of the rewards for our work. We own the union, we operate it, and we aren't going to screw ourselves. Better yet, start your own small local business, with family and friends, owned locally and cooperatively. The giant corporations that have been able to compete unfairly through government subsidies and cheap, subsidized energy are dinosaurs. The future is small, local, and cooperative.

Does your local supermarket offer only genetically modified, supersized, flavorless, unnaturally colored food laced with poisonous chemicals — all so they will endure shipping and have a long shelf life? Huge, privately held, transnational corporations located who knows where, owned by who knows who, doing who knows what to your food, taking unfairly large profits out of your local community are the illness. Creating and joining a local, democratic food co-op, keeping the money flowing in your own neighborhood, is the liberal dose of economic democracy that cures it. We own it, we operate it, and we aren't going to poison ourselves. We'll ensure that we carry reasonably priced organic produce from local farms. Another good, liberal dose is buying directly from the local organic family farmer. She's not going to poison us either.

Creating and maintaining labor unions, credit unions, and food co-ops takes time and effort, and direct democracy can get very messy and frustrating. Some of the most uncooperative people I've ever worked with are in the cooperative movement. But these institutions are based on real democracy, with real people grappling with real issues, trying to make community work fairly, equitably, and with justice for all.

Donating to the Future

The justice and economic equitability that a true democratic society offers come at a price. True democracy takes our most precious personal resources, time and money, and turns them into justice and equality. When we can't be bothered to give our time to make our democracy really work, we're going to get screwed. When we insist on always trying to get the cheapest price, someone else is going to get screwed.

Creating, operating, and supporting local, democratic economic institutions, whether it is a credit union, labor union, consumer co-op, producer co-op, small local farm, or small local business, takes time. Writing and visiting elected officials and protesting illegal wars take time — time away from family, creative pursuits, and travel. Consider it a donation to justice and the future. Consider it Soul School, a way to find meaning and do meaningful work.

Supporting local farms and small businesses also takes money. Cheap food, cheap clothing, cheap stuff ride on the backs of workers, whether it's a disabled veteran begging nickels on the corner, a laid-off professional standing in line at the food bank, a hungry child in a farmworker labor camp, or an Asian farmer forced off his land to work for peanuts making our shoes. The local organic farmer is not subsidized by our tax dollars like the huge corporate farmer making profits from those taxes and from the labor-saving poisons sprayed on the food we'll eat. Her food gives us health, not cancer. Her farm sustains the land instead of using it up. Supporting her may cost a bit more. Consider it a donation to justice and to our health and future. Consider it Soul School, a way to find meaning and support meaningful work.

Creative Action Hero

Back in the seventies, I met a guy named Bill Leland who had built three dome homes up on Skyline Ridge near Palo Alto. My family was living in a small cabin on the edge of a ranch nearby, and Bill invited us to live in one of the domes when it was vacated. Bill's family lived in one dome, our family in another, and the third dome was used as the common kitchen and dining area. Living in close proximity with others allows you not only to experience the ups and downs of cooperative living but also to get to know a person's real character and lived values. I developed a deep admiration for the life and character of Bill Leland. This is a man who lives and works his values every day.

After completing most of his course work toward a doctorate in educational psychology at Stanford University, Bill went on to serve as cofounder and executive director of several pioneering nonprofits involved with environmental, peace, social justice, and economic justice issues. In the past few years he has been the director of community development for the progressive and innovative Santa Cruz Community Credit Union. The credit union community extends from the faculty, students, and surfers around the University of California in Santa Cruz south to the farmers' fields and farmworker barrios of John Steinbeck's novels, around Watsonville, Salinas, and Monterey.

It's not often that we ask our friends about their values and beliefs and why they think like they do. It's almost a forbidden topic, like asking about their net worth. But I did ask Bill, and what a privilege to hear a caring, thoughtful man who has dedicated his life to community service describe what motivates him and why. Here's what he had to say:

We humans define our own and our collective purposes. My purpose is to take good care of the physical vehicle I have been given; to love myself, those who I touch directly, and those who I touch indirectly — all sentient beings; to do as little harm as possible to the physical world — to love the physical world; and, to be of service. The manifestation of love is service.

I find meaning through connection with people, connection with the natural world, and through service. My work is to promote social and economic justice through focusing on community economic development that serves underserved people and that serves the community collectively. This work is done to serve low-income people by developing asset building tools and incentives, by providing financial education, by increasing affordable, quality child care, by encouraging socially, environmentally, and economically responsible businesses, and the like.

To the extent that I can provide real service and contribute to fundamental change of the dominant systems in our U.S. society, I am useful.

*I am passionate about giving whatever encouragement and support
I can to people who have been abused, oppressed, neglected, or denied
opportunities, so that they can believe in themselves, become empowered,
and gain skills and access to resources in order to experience a high quality of life based in dignity, happiness, and love.*

*I try, through various, occasional practices and daily reminders, to
be more in touch with the spiritual world, with the universal spirit, with
the energy that flows through all of life, with the affirmation of life and
vitality. I try to hold a sense of the beauty and love in life and the natural world while also holding a consciousness of the suffering in the world.
I believe that we human beings have only barely touched the tremendous
potential that we have in all aspects of our lives.*

Bill exemplifies democratic values lived. As distinguished from
the Action Heroes offered to us in myth, legend, and popular culture,
taking on their enemies with weapons of destruction, *Creative* Action
Heroes are those who do meaningful work serving and building their
community, their only weapons being active love, dedication, and
brainpower.

Cesar Chavez and Me

"When we are really honest with ourselves," Cesar Chavez once
said, "we must admit our lives are all that really belong to us. So it is
how we use our lives that determines the kind of men we are.... Our
cause goes on in hundreds of distant places. It multiplies among
thousands and then millions of caring people who heed through a
multitude of simple deeds the commandment set out in the book of
the prophet Micah, in the Old Testament: 'What does the Lord
require of you, but to do justice, to love kindness, and to walk
humbly with your God.'"

While my dad was building a church, Cesar Chavez was building a union. My dad believed that by winning others to his belief system, he was building himself a mansion in heaven on a street paved

with gold. Cesar was living and organizing for a better life for farm-workers in a San Jose barrio called Sal Si Puedes, which means "Escape If You Can."

What I loved most about the farmworkers' movement when Cesar asked me to join in 1968 was our complete and utter absorption in the cause. The work consumed our everyday lives 24/7, and it had real meaning. I had gone from work that was, for me, soul-less and dispiriting to work that was meaningful; from systems analysis and writing computer code in order to support weapons systems and make the distribution of cars more efficient, to learning about nonviolence and direct action, walking picket lines, and hiring programmers to write computer code that mattered, that had meaning. My work was now helping make the world a better place for the lowly, not through charity, but by helping them find the power of their own organization and their own voice.

Synchronicity

My main responsibility with the United Farm Workers Union (UFW) was to design and implement a computerized system for the union's service center to run the membership, credit union, and medical services. Some Stanford MBA candidates and their professors had designed a computer system for the union, and the union had just started looking for someone to implement it for them. My job application to become a community organizer arrived there at just the right time. They saw my background in computer systems development and invited me to join them at headquarters to head up the project.

The Stanford people had designed a good system based on text-books and theory, but I had to redesign it for the real world of business that I knew. I hired four computer programmers who came to work for room and board and five dollars a week, like the rest of us. We developed bilingual reports for use at the service center offices that would be available to the migrant farmworkers who followed the harvest from Southern California to Washington State. When we needed to work on political campaigns, we would pack up and move to a city as a team, organize and campaign, then return and resume the work we'd left behind.

One of my projects with the UFW was working on member registration with Dolores Huerta, who was the cofounder with Cesar and is now first vice president emeritus. The mother of eleven children, fourteen grandchildren, and four great-grandchildren, Dolores is a smart, fiery dynamo who negotiated the first union contracts in 1966 and spoke out against the toxic pesticides that threaten farmworkers, consumers, and the environment. These early union contracts required growers to stop using such dangerous pesticides as DDT and parathion. She also directed the UFW's national grape boycott, taking the plight of the farmworkers to the consumers. As a result of the boycott, the entire California table grape industry signed a three-year collective bargaining agreement with the UFW. Dolores has more than paid her dues; she's been arrested twenty-two times for nonviolent peaceful union activities.

The growing success of the UFW was challenged in 1970 by the Teamsters Union, which saw an opportunity to gain contracts in "sweetheart deals" with growers who did not want to deal with the growing effectiveness of the Chicano worker–led Farm Workers Union. In the process, the UFW lost many of the contracts it had worked so long and hard to obtain, and with them, much of its dues-paying membership, which had peaked at seventy thousand. As the conflict of union against union got hot and heavy, I volunteered to work as a soundman on a film about the union, *Fighting for Our Lives*, which later was nominated for an Academy Award. The producer/cameraman and I posed as TV station reporters from Bakersfield to get footage from behind the Teamster lines, out in the fields. We thought we were pretty clever until we were told that a carload of Teamster goons with baseball bats had found out we were actually from the union and were hunting for us. Not wanting to test our nonviolent mettle at that particular time, we left town.

Ideals Meet Real Life

You never know just how you will stand up to injustice until it happens, until you are actually confronted with a life-or-death situation that tests your idealistic, and theoretical, commitment to nonviolence.

In 1969 we had moved the headquarters for the UFW from Delano, California, to the hills above Bakersfield near the town of Tehachapi, where my son, Josh, was born. A former tuberculosis sanitarium had been purchased by a Hollywood movie producer and donated to the union. The compound of ramshackle buildings and mobile homes was named "La Paz," but the peace was shattered several times daily by freight trains running through the grounds.

Because of previous threats to his life, Cesar was forced to live with twenty-four-hour bodyguards and two trained German shepherd guard dogs he named Boycott and Huelga (Spanish for "strike"). He also traveled in a two-car convoy. As problems escalated between the two unions, we began hearing rumors, verified by the police, that the Mafia had put out a contract on Cesar's life and planned to rub him out. At a meeting called by the head of security, we learned that law enforcement had notified us that La Paz could be invaded, with the goal of killing Cesar. We were given guns and ammo to keep in our homes, and we began taking target practice with revolvers and shotguns at the nearby shooting range maintained by the local police department. We took turns standing watch with the regular security staff, driving around the perimeter of the grounds throughout the night.

Needless to say, this armed response to threat conflicted with the philosophy of nonviolence espoused by the union, and by most of us personally. I was puzzled at the lack of any challenges to this policy — including my own silence. Our families, our movement, and our leader were being threatened, and we were preparing to defend ourselves by violent means, regardless of our philosophical dedication to nonviolence. Did that mean justice is only ultimately possible through the barrel of a gun as Chairman Mao famously stated, that our own reality was like the Old West after all? Were we helplessly weak and naive to believe in values that, when push came to shove, we would simply give up? Would we really regress back to force rather than live our ideals, no matter what? What was the responsible thing to do?

Although I regularly worked with Cesar and his wife, Helen, I was not part of the inner circle that made major policy decisions. I don't know personally whether Cesar knew about the arming of headquarters staff, but I assume he did. In any case, knowing him, I am quite certain he would never have made such a decision in order to save his own life. Rather, it would have been a responsible decision made to save the union and the people he cared for. When Gandhi was killed, his movement died. When King was killed, his movement lost its momentum. Cesar was not going to let that happen to his movement and the hopes and dreams of farmworkers, even if it meant his personal beliefs were violated. As for me, although my Tolstoyan/Gandhian idealism died a little death during this experience, my admiration for Cesar grew because of it. I say, good for him. I loved him for that.

This brief episode of armed vigilance ended suddenly one day, when the guard at the front gate of our compound apparently got into an argument with a rancher who had access rights through the property. As the incident was described to me, the argument escalated and the guard pulled a shotgun and leveled it at the rancher. No shots were fired, but as the reality of what could go wrong when loaded guns are available to poorly trained volunteers sank in, it became too obvious a risk to continue. All the guns were quietly confiscated, and we once more became nonviolent pacifists.

As human and fallible as anyone, Chavez was resolute and unyielding in his determination to find justice for his cause. Just as strong were the virtues of compassion and humility he demonstrated in his personal relationships with friend and foe alike. He believed in life, liberty, and the pursuit of happiness for everyone, not just a chosen few or those in authority. Like Gandhi, when he asked for sacrifice he was willing to make the biggest personal sacrifices himself. It was my honor to have known and worked with him.

A union of poor people working together to better their lives takes a true leap of faith — into the arms and hearts of each other. Only by believing in each other, working with each other, caring for each other is anything worthwhile accomplished. Justice, democracy, peace, time, and money walk hand in hand into our shared future. A just, equitable distribution of resources comes only with an economic democracy made real and true by our commitment of personal time and money to make it work for us. And when it works, true economic democracy brings peace.

What are the character traits of those who have faith in each other, who hope for a bright future not only for themselves but for everyone, and who understand that justice and democracy are the keys to that future? As we've seen, they are generous, unselfish, warmhearted, openhanded, receptive, freely giving, benevolent, and tolerant. Would you say that's a good list? Would you like to have someone like that as a friend or coworker? I keyed those words into my online dictionary. They are synonyms for, and definitions of, a word that has been besmirched and much belittled of late:

Liberal.

Meaningful work comes alive
When justice acts from care and compassion.
And that requires temperance....

temperance

[the briarpatch way]

·

Wisdom demands a new orientation of science and technology towards the organic, the gentle, the non-violent, the elegant and beautiful.

— E. F. Schumacher

To live meaningfully is to be at perpetual risk.

— Robert McKee

Most people prefer no work at all to meaningless work, or wasted work, or made work....If work is meaningless, then life comes close to being meaningless.

— Abraham Maslow

D
o you find your work meaningful? Do you go to work each day looking forward to seeing the members of your team? Does what you're doing feel useful to you?

Temperance means to be moderate in one's needs and to show restraint in one's actions. E. F. Schumacher identifies temperance as "knowing when enough is enough." Temperance is usually interpreted as a stern, drab self-denial. But it can also mean the acceptance that on this tiny planet we share, some of us have been taking *much more* than our equitable share, directly and indirectly resulting in *much less* of an equitable share for others. ("Equitable" does not mean "equal"; it means a fair, just, and reasonable share.)

According to *AdBusters* magazine: "The World Values Survey of sixty-five countries found that Nigeria (fifty-fifth in the world for GDP) has the highest percentage of happy people, whereas the U.S. (number one for GDP) ranks sixteenth and the UK twenty-fourth. Why so low? According to *New Scientist* magazine, 'Survey after survey has shown that the desire for material goods, which has increased hand in hand with average income, is a happiness suppressant.'"

Lack of temperance feeds greed, the lowest form of ambition, which aggravates conflict and leads us to reject diplomatic solutions and instead invest in arms races and military solutions. Temperance, on the other hand, allows us to reduce hostility by working cooperatively, which in turn allows us to reduce our firepower and to invest in alternative energy sources, education, and health rather than in weaponry.

Temperance is a virtue we choose for ourselves, not something we impose on others. It is sometimes associated with self-denial and being grimly conservative, but I think it's much more at home with liberality. When one is personally temperate, one can more afford to be openhearted and generous with others.

Temperance means quality rather than quantity. The more stuff we make and have, the less each item is honored in and of itself.

Ready access to the zillions of this and that, cheaply made on industrial assembly lines, lessens our ability to want and treasure, or even afford, that which is carefully and honorably made. In Robert Pirsig's *Zen and the Art of Motorcycle Maintenance: An Inquiry into Values*, first published in 1974, he writes: "It is the little, pathetic attempts at Quality that kill. The plaster false fireplace in the apartment, shaped and waiting to contain a flame that can never exist. Or the hedge in front of the apartment building with a few square feet of grass behind it. A few square feet of grass... If they just left out the hedge and grass it would be all right. Now it serves only *to draw attention to what has been lost.*" (Italics added.) He goes on:

[I]f he takes whatever dull job he's stuck with... and they are all, sooner or later, dull... and, just to keep himself amused, starts to look for options of Quality, and secretly pursues these options, just for their own sake, thus making an art out of what he is doing, he's likely to discover that he becomes a much more interesting person and much less of an object to the people around him because his Quality decisions change him too. And not only the job and him, but others too because the Quality tends to fan out like waves. The Quality job he didn't think anyone was going to see is seen and the person who sees it feels a little better because of it, and is likely to pass that feeling on to others, and in that way the Quality tends to keep on going. My personal feeling is that this is how any further improvement of the world will be done: by individuals making Quality decisions and that's all.

In 1979 I cofounded a company that was about Quality, in Pirsig's sense of the word.

Smith & Hawken

As you read earlier, Alan Chadwick had come to the University of California at Santa Cruz and turned a rocky hillside into a garden paradise. His basic tools were a garden spade and garden fork that Smith & Hawken began importing, along with other garden implements, from Bulldog Tools in Wigan, England, where tools had been hand forged for over two hundred years. Their original foundry was where the first garden fork had been invented and forged. Bulldog Tools had kept its reputation for offering the finest, toughest garden tools available in a culture that honored and practiced gardening.

Chadwick's gardening method required "double-digging" using a fork and spade. By digging down and loosening the soil a couple of feet deep, he was able to plant very densely, so that as the plants matured, their leaves would touch each other. This creates a soil-cooling miniclimate beneath the plants, keeping the soil moist and loose and producing much more per square foot of land than normal, with much less water. By the late seventies some of Chadwick's apprentices were moving on to start their own gardens and small farm projects. Needing Bulldog Tools themselves, they had been importing a few at a time at great expense.

The American throwaway culture had robbed us of good, well-made tools. It seemed consumers only wanted the cheapest and latest design available. Next year there would be an improved, cheaper version, so why spend money on quality? Consequently, if a weekend gardener needed to do vigorous work in heavy clay soil, their hardware variety ten-dollar fork would either bend under pressure or the handle would break, and it would be tossed aside in frustration. A serious, seasoned gardener was also helpless and continuously frustrated with tools that could not do the job.

But we didn't know if there would be a market for tools that cost four times as much, even if they did last a lifetime. We hadn't done any focus groups. We only knew that we and our friends wanted these tools, and homegrown market research hinted at a market with potential. But it seemed like quality as a concept was pretty much dead. Lowest price had trumped everything.

There was a small market among these Chadwick gardeners, and we could run this company part-time while we also worked at other things, so we brought our first half-container load over and started a business. We tried wholesaling the tools in local, upscale garden nurseries, but knowledgeable, enthusiastic salespeople were required to tell the story of their quality and the lost idea that it was less expensive in the long term to buy something that would last, rather than buy something cheaper that would have to be continually repurchased. When I dropped by one of the stores and found our tools stashed and neglected in a corner, gathering dust, that was it. We discontinued the wholesale route and decided to sell the tools directly to customers by mail order, in our own tiny storefront, and eventually in our own stores. We cared about quality, and we could tell the story in a catalog and over the phone. Once we mailed the catalog and the phone started ringing, we realized we had struck a nerve and there was a much bigger market than we had imagined. People were actually hungry for quality. They got our message about sturdy tools that would last, and we started working full-time to meet the demand. When our first employee, Ann, took an order, hung up the phone, and started yelling, "I just talked to Harrison Ford!! I just talked to Harrison Ford!!" we knew we'd arrived.

What we learned was that our company had to live up to the quality of the tools we were selling. The craft and workmanship passed on and still honored and practiced in Wigan, England, at Bulldog's Clarington Forge — hard, hot, sweaty, dangerous foundry work requiring skill and attention — demanded our own attention to quality in all that we did. Our customers, admiring and using well-designed tools perfectly fitted to the work, expected the same quality from us. Our employees, who worked with us because they were attracted to the tools and to the company selling them, also expected it. If we didn't live up to the tools, in the quality of our catalog, in our customer service, in our guarantee (forever), in our daily actions together as a team, then we would be dishonoring the gift of good work done well by hundreds of workers, over hundreds of years.

Several years ago, long after I had left, Smith & Hawken management got into a spat with Bulldog and allowed their exclusive arrangement to end. When I heard this, I called Bulldog immediately and began selling their tools at Seeds of Change, where you can still find them under the Clarington Forge brand. There are some clever knockoffs of Bulldog tools, made in Asia and sold by various companies, but the head is not forged from one piece of metal, which, along with the carefully selected Ash handles, are what make Bulldog forks and spades so strong. Instead, they are welded together, ground down, and painted to look like real, hand-forged tools. The Smith, and the Hawken, and the Bulldog Tools are all long gone, so I don't know what quality means anymore at the company I helped to found, or where the garden tools they now sell are manufactured.

During the early years, I think the company lived up to and exceeded the expectations of our customers, as high as they were. Our service, like the quality of our tools, was legendary. But internally, we sucked. The company culture evolved into a disaster, badly welded together and not matched up to the character of our tools. Like the Bulldog knockoffs, or Pirsig's few square feet of grass, we only looked like the real thing. And that only "draws attention to what has been lost."

What Work Once Was

"We have known workmen who really wanted to work," the French author Charles Peguy wrote.

No one thought of anything but work. We have known workmen who in the morning thought of nothing but work. They got up in the morning (and at what an hour), and they sang at the idea that they were off to work. At eleven o'clock they sang on going off to eat their soup. Work for them was joy itself and the deep root of their being. And the reason of their being. There was an incredible honor in work, the most beautiful of all the honors...perhaps the only one which stands of itself....

A chair rung had to be well made. That was an understood thing.
That was the first thing. It wasn't that the chair rung had to be well made
for the salary or on account of the salary. It wasn't that it was well made
for the boss, nor for connoisseurs, nor for the boss's clients. It had to be
well made itself, in itself, for itself, in its very self. A tradition coming,
springing from deep within the race; a history, an absolute, an honor,
demanded that this chair rung be well made. Every part of the chair
which could not be seen was just as perfectly made as the parts which
could be seen.... There was no question of being seen or of not being seen.
It was the innate being of work which needed to be well done.

Quality has always been closely associated with skill, attention to detail, and building with the best materials. But what about use? What about value to the community? To be something of Quality, are these necessary too?

Ends and Means

The language of business has undergone a transition. It is no longer what you make and how you make it, but how what you make is used that identifies your contribution to the world — and this is as it should be. For instance, a company will identify itself with "We're in the cooking business" rather than "We make pots and pans." Unfortunately, such language is often used as hyperbole and misdirection rather than making clear what a company does.

To determine what is useful and meaningful work one must of necessity start with the output and its usefulness. As an example, let's follow Joe to work this morning. Joe receives a great salary that supports a lovely family living in a typical suburb with good schools. He goes to work each day in a new car, walks to a nice new building, and arrives in his large corner office with beautiful mahogany desk and credenza. His company's factory is on the other side of town, where the noise and smells and wastes are problems for its immediate neighborhood and the workers at the plant, but not for him or the headquarters staff. His daily reports are carefully organized in neat piles for his perusal and decision making. He does quality work that results in the best quality product in his industry. His bright, cheerful secretary brings in his coffee. His best friend down the hall stops in to say good morning. He is looking forward to meeting his wife for lunch at the new cool restaurant in town. Everyone and everything is right with Joe's world. This was what was promised to him as he studied and worked so long and hard to make it. He is now set and life is great. Joe will spend the rest of his day doing his regular great job producing the best possible product for his many customers.

Does Joe have meaningful work? Let's look at the output. His company makes cigarettes. Its tagline, using the new language of business, may be something like "Our business is pleasure," but they are really in the killing business. Their true tagline should be "We kill our customers." Is that work with meaning?

Context is everything. The end result of what we do — its effect on others and on our common ground — is how we judge useful and meaningful work. To be responsible is to be responsible for the consequences as well as for the means. Good quality work is harmful if the end result of the work is harmful. Not only is Joe producing harmful products, but to continue as a profitable concern and for Joe to do the best job he possibly can, his company must replace its dead customers by recruiting more to kill. The more customers he and his company can convince to buy their product, even though it will kill them, the more his company will prosper, the "healthier" its bottom line will be. Even though the gurneys with the dead and dying will not be rolled through the halls of his elegant office building or show up on his spreadsheets (except as the rapidly increasing costs for liability insurance), Joe cannot ignore the end result of his quality work by pleading nonresponsibility for how others use his product. He's responsible for making sure they *do* use it.

Let's take another example. A bomb-making company is not in the business of simply making metal things that explode, things that sit there unused, accumulating storage costs, waiting to defend the country. That would be a money loser. They're not doing their jobs unless they're increasing their profits for their shareholders. Their company is in the business of killing and destroying. Making sure the bombs get dropped on someone so replacements can be made to increase profits is their business. Their tagline should be: "We make war." They may also have a subsidiary company that comes into bombed-out countries to rebuild — what we might call double-dip profiteering.

Do you find meaning in the end results of your work? Does your work enhance life or harm it? If you're an engineer, is it more meaningful to design bridges, or bombs? If you're in the health profession, is it more meaningful to recommend nutrition, or drugs? If you're a farmer, is it more meaningful to pour chemicals that cause cancer on food, or work with nature to produce clean and healthy food? What is the end result of what we spend our days doing? Does our work enhance life or harm it?

When life and work are meaningless, peace is not possible. Violence hovers around a meaningless life twitching its tail like a cat watching a mouse hole. To become fully human, with our souls intact, is our most important task. When we are making progress and our values fully agree with our work, we become fully engaged and meaning is ever present in our daily lives.

The relationship to our work, something that many of us are engaged in for well over half of our waking hours, changes for the worse if we are spending all that precious time involved in something we don't respect or that even damages our communities or our own families. Not only don't we have meaningful work, but worse yet, we are spending our time destructively. We turn our feelings off, deaden them with the various escape devices so prevalent in our turned-off world, and erect a gradually hardening shell of denial and despair, painted over with the cheerful countenance demanded by human resource departments to fit in. This kills the spirit, or at least puts it into hibernation until five o'clock.

A recent published survey showed that 48 percent of retail workers say they do not look forward to going to work each day. Fifty-four percent of retail workers say they are dissatisfied with their paychecks. Forty-eight percent of retail workers feel excessive stress on the job due to the demands of their customers, employers, and families. Forty-seven percent of retail workers say finding a new job is on their list of New Year's resolutions.

The Phone Never Stops

Trapped in a dead-end job at a customer service call center, a man in his mid-thirties hears the ringing and just doesn't care. In the online magazine *Salon*, he described his experiences in this meaningless job, taking orders and customer complaints for books that, unbeknownst to customers, wouldn't be delivered for weeks. "Here, there were always calls waiting, always telephones buzzing with urgent anger. Customers barely holding in their contempt, scarcely masking their disappointment in the poor quality of necessary human interaction they have just inherited, toll-free.…

"The phone does not stop. Problems, catalogs, orders, ringing, ringing, ringing. The phone *does not stop*."

Thinking he can make an impression and get a promotion, he puts together a list of ideas for how things can be improved and made more efficient, but he hears nothing back and nothing is done. When he asks why, he is told that his suggestions had all been tried previously, and none of them worked. "And that's the day I officially stopped caring. Never stay late. Never work overtime. Never offer opinions. Do *not* go the extra mile. The *phones don't stop*.…I don't want to take calls anymore. I'm afraid I'm going to die this way. The phone's 'heavy queue' light is blinking. There are fourteen calls on hold, waiting for us. For me." He then begins subtle sabotage by picking up the phone occasionally but not saying anything, just leaving empty air for the customer. As he listens to the customers stew and scream, he feels that by playing this cruel joke he's somehow saving himself. "And *the phone does not stop*."

In 1972, Studs Terkel published his great book *Working*. He interviewed about a hundred workers across the United States, and most of them seemed to echo the sentiments of this help-desk worker. There's the cosmetics salesperson who would like to do "something more vital" and make a contribution; the auditor who doesn't have much to say about his unexciting work: "I could say, 'Wow, I saw this company yesterday and their balance sheet, wow!' There just isn't much to talk about"; the stockbroker: "I'd like one morning to wake up and go to some work that gave me joy"; the editor: "[M]ost of us are looking for a calling, not a job. . . . Jobs are not big enough for people"; the government bureaucrat: "The most frustrating thing for me is to know that what I'm doing does not have a positive impact on others. I don't see this work as meaning anything." Then there's the community organizer: "I'm one of the few people in life who was lucky enough to find out what he really wanted to do. I'm just havin' a ball, the time of my life. I feel sorry for all these people I run across all the time who aren't doing what they want to do. Their lives are hell. You've got one life. You've got, say, sixty-five years. How on earth can you blow forty-five years of that doing something you hate?"

In It for the Meaning

So how does temperance help us find this sort of work? If you are moderate in your needs and don't see success as maximizing income and material possessions, you gain more freedom to take risks, to raise values and meaning to the top of your work requirements, and be more selective about the companies you work for. As I mentioned in the introduction, Abraham Maslow was a pioneer in the field of humanistic psychology, a revolutionary resurrection of traditional wisdom into secular culture. He was best known for his theory of the hierarchy of needs and his concept of self-actualization as our highest motivating force. A refreshing alternative to the behaviorists and Freudians, his enlightened psychology formed part of the foundation of the human potential movement. His research was concerned with what is most uniquely human and healthy, rather than what humanity shares with animals, or what is wrong with us. He believed that the proper management of people in the workplace can improve them and their lives, and in turn improve the world.

For Maslow, the path to human happiness was best found through worthwhile work. Virtue comes naturally to people — creativity, compassion, fairness, justice, responsibility — if the environment and context of their work are set up to encourage this. Good management starts with what you feel about people. Are they fundamentally good and trustworthy? Would they rather work than not work? Do they want to find meaning in their work? If you assume the best, get the business basics right, and also create an open, shared, team-oriented workplace, you will be rewarded with a thriving, profitable business. If you assume the worst, then you create an authoritarian, hierarchical organization that can never reach its fullest potential, or true financial success, because the company does not allow the people in it to reach their fullest potential. And ultimately, if democratic values are not brought into the workplace, then democracy itself is threatened.

Self-actualized people don't have jobs, they have callings, a mission. They care about values and purpose. They want to work for a company that values them as individuals, not as conformists. Maslow taught very pragmatic management, saying that the reason to manage a company humanistically is because it works better. And research has borne him out: friendly, compassionate, nonauthoritarian companies with enlightened management are more profitable.

Management theorist Douglas McGregor developed the concepts of Theory X and Theory Y behavior, echoing much of what Maslow wrote. Theory X assumes that people are dependent and don't want to work, and that getting work out of them requires management to either inspire or threaten. Theory Y assumes that people are self-motivated to work and want to be part of something worthwhile that they can feel good committing themselves to. Management's role then becomes coaching, making sure that communications are open and functioning, making sure results are being fed back appropriately, and then getting out of the way.

These ideas had a real impact. During the sixties and seventies, along with the social upheavals going on that challenged the status quo assumptions about our lives and work, the human potential movement was fomenting a democratic revolution in the workplace. Why was there such an emphasis on competition and survival of the fittest when research, even by Darwin himself, showed that evolution is also a process of cooperation and mutual aid? As humans and human societies evolved, human emotions also evolved, adding idealism, generosity, and other altruistic behaviors to the social mix. Wouldn't businesses that established management practices based on collaboration and teamwork attract the best and brightest and give them a competitive advantage in the process?

McGregor emphasized values. He taught that people want their companies to stand for something, and that they will give their best when they are working in common cause for something they can believe in, a product or cause that means something to them. They want to be trusted and honored as adults and to be brought into the decision-making process.

McGregor's most enduring legacy may be the practice of Open Book Management. This practice evolved out of the experiments in management that his theories of trust and openness sparked. Open Book Management opens the financial records and reports to everyone within the company as a way of involving them and sharing responsibility for results. Jack Stack famously used Open Book Management to build the Springfield Remanufacturing Corporation. In his book *The Great Game of Business*, Stack writes: "The best, most efficient, most profitable way to operate a business is to give everybody in the company a voice in saying how the company is run and a stake in the financial outcome, good or bad.... A business should be run like an aquarium, where everybody can see what's going on — what's going in, what's moving around, what's coming out. That's the only way to make sure people understand what you're doing, and why, and have some input into deciding where you are going. Then, when the unexpected happens, they know how to react and react quickly."

I might add that when a company is open and transparent about numbers, giving everyone a say about operations, the shared value system of the entire workforce becomes the value system of *the company* rather than just top management. Workers who live in the community are more apt to raise questions about practices that could be harmful to their community than are managers who are more attuned to the financial implications.

Unfortunately, many managers and entrepreneurs continue to operate with coercion, fear, and distrust rather than compassion. This is true across the spectrum, be it in small start-ups or MegaMaws.

Even though research has well proven that companies with good values are more profitable, the research usually does not factor in the context and end result of a company's business. A company is judged solely on its financial success, under the assumption that "the market" should be left unfettered by values. Being more democratic, team-oriented, and humanistic internally, and therefore more profitable, can work for a cigarette company just as well as a solar energy company. As McGregor acknowledged, this definition of meaning at work needs to be broadened to include a company's values about the context and the effect of what it does beyond the company itself.

For a lot of people, having good internal company values is extremely important, even sufficient in itself. I suppose one can thrive in a company culture that rewards good work and be proud to work for, say, Coca-Cola. It's a world-class brand that's number one in its industry. But what real value does selling caffeinated sugar water bring to the world? Is it positive, negative, or neutral? What is the effect on customers' health? What is the context? What is the result of the product and its use? Are there any values added? And, further, what is the result of its marketing and dominance in third world countries? Why have labor organizers apparently been killed inside their Colombia plants while organizing? Who is responsible? What is the responsibility of other employees in the company when their company stands accused of reprehensible behavior? Ignore it? Research it? Does the company operate openly with nothing to hide and make sure its employees are fully informed about its operating values?

Creating Values-Added Work

The United Farm Workers Union, where I was able to put my skills to work for a cause I believe in, spoiled me for any regular job I may have found upon returning to the Bay Area in 1973. My wife and I had survived for four years on room and board and five dollars a week, produced our first child, and had the time of our lives. In the process I had transferred my father's sense of mission, that of saving souls for an assumed afterlife in heaven, to a here-and-now social mission. Helping to better the lives of poor, hardworking people had purpose and value for me, and I now *required* a job with meaning.

Nonprofit work was one way to go, but the nonprofits I'd observed had the same laid-back nonchalance of government and academic workplaces. For some, a library-like atmosphere of hushed calm and unhurried camaraderie is the soothing environment they feel comfortable in. For others, it can be boring. I wanted the *in*temperate action, the daily drama, the battle for survival, the electric sense of urgency, and the sometimes sheer craziness that I'd found so exuberantly fulfilling as part of the UFW. The challenge, as I saw it, was to find or develop a work situation that created value and competed in the real world of commerce and that also had a social mission to help make a positive difference in the world.

I knocked around at a couple of jobs that were deadening beyond belief until some friends started talking up a small cooperative natural foods store. Values, mission, risk, social change — all were being discussed as part of the real world of making a business work. That was what I was looking for.

The Briarpatch Network

During the seventies and eighties, two businesses I cofounded, Briarpatch Cooperative Market and Smith & Hawken, were members of the Briarpatch Network, an informal business association centered in San Francisco. The network was a group of like-minded small-business owners who shared ideas and values about business. I also cofounded a branch of the network on the San Francisco Peninsula, soon to become famous as Silicon Valley, and met weekly with small local businesses at Jesse Cool's Late for the Train restaurant in Menlo Park. We were a thriving community that shared expertise and resources in the best tradition of mutual aid, and that periodically got together to square dance and whoop it up.

One key to Briarpatch values was the ability to live on less. By participating in a community that supported and valued frugality and rejected the symbols of material success and conformity that demanded one's participation in their acquisition, we gained the freedom to experiment with alternative ways of doing business. In short, changing the rules of the game made the game a lot more fun. Radical political analysis had taught us the direct connection between the bombs we were dropping on other people and the materialist addictions of our culture. But rather than just protesting and picketing, we were creating new, alternative models for human livelihood. Along with these values, we embraced voluntary simplicity in our personal habits, living conditions, and buying patterns, which made it possible to focus less time on generating income to pay the bills. Crucial to living and working simply is the support of a community whose values we can, in return, admire and support. It includes the practical sharing of mutual needs and resources. Rather than each member storing a growing heap of possessions in the garage or storage unit, the community itself became the repository of items not immediately needed, with objects circulated through active exchange and barter.

The Briarpatch Society was conceptualized in 1973 by Dick Raymond, a Harvard Business School graduate who gave up a successful conventional business career to create small nonprofits and other ventures, including the Portola Institute, a catalyst for several community-based groups and the first publisher of the revolutionary *Whole Earth Catalog*.

The Briarpatch Society consisted of people learning to "live with joy in the cracks," Raymond says in *The Briarpatch Book*. "But, more particularly, if you are positively oriented and doing (or actively seeking) Right Livelihood, even willing to fail young, and concerned with the sharing of resources and skills with members of an ongoing community (or affinity group), and especially if you see yourself as part of a subsociety that is more committed to 'learning how the world works' than to acquiring possessions and status, then you must be a *Briar*."

Dick's Briarpatch idea grew out of a time of doom and gloom, social tumult, value questioning, and high unemployment, a time when the demise of big business seemed imminent. He saw the giant corporate dinosaurs unable to find food for their enormous profit-oriented appetites. He visualized a business apocalypse. He envisioned the Briarpatch as the social system for survival. Briars would use the tools of living on less, sharing with each other, and learning through new small businesses. To this, Dick added the positive value of doing it all with joy. In his vision, Briars were to be doing what they loved most, secure from the ravages of the crumbling culture around them. Their lack of material possessions and small-scale living would appear to others like real briar patches — thorny places so unappealing to the greedy people around them that, like Br'er Rabbit, Briars would be safe.

Another key for many of us was, and still is, the Buddhist concept of "right livelihood" — not right in the sense of conforming to a definition of right versus wrong, but right in that each of us is unique and has a distinctive contribution to make that is right for us and right for the community we participate in. New models of living and working that hearkened back to the utopians of previous generations appealed to our values and enthusiasm for experimentation. *The Lord of the Rings* trilogy was popular reading, and the philosophy of Dick's hobbitlike Briarpatch Society repudiated and replaced the values of the society we were disillusioned with. Briarpatch values continue to live in many hearts, and some of its management practices have been successfully incorporated in businesses far and wide. A Briarpatch Cooperative Market still thrives in Grass Valley, California. (For more on the history, the businesses involved, and ongoing evolution of the Briarpatch Network, please see www.briarpatch.net and www.briarpatchcoop.com.)

The seventies predictions of devastating energy shortages were only briefly manifest, and the giant corporate MegaMaws are still gulping down large swaths of business terrain, expanding into all the world to preach the gospel of raw capitalism. The day of reckoning has been postponed, yet the signs of serious difficulties ahead continue to be manifest.

Briarpatch Management

For Briarpatch businesses, mutual aid and the free exchange of knowledge and equipment allow small businesses to open with very little capital. Some of them have also been financed by their customers through direct public offerings (DPOs) and other innovative financing (see, for example, www.diamondorganicsshares.com).

Central to Briarpatch values of openness and sharing is the practice of Open Book Management that McGregor promoted in his work. Indeed, Briarpatch businesses took the concept further than McGregor would have imagined. Unlike the financial statements of publicly traded corporations that, by law, publish summaries of their finances for investors, the Briarpatch concept of open books means that the everyday bookkeeping of the company is available to employees, customers, neighbors, *and* competitors. Anyone can walk into a Briarpatch business and ask to see the books. You can find out not only what the income and expenses of the business are, but also (horror of horrors) what the owners and employees take in salary, how much the company is spending for advertising and with whom they spend it, how much is paid in taxes, and so on. Every line item is available for scrutiny. This practice comes from the idea that a business is responsible to the community it serves. Its wage structure and resource allocation should be justifiable; the business practices it espouses should be verifiable.

This sounds pretty radical today, but up until the late 1800s, all corporate behavior was subject to political control through their state representatives. States created the corporate charters that companies operated under and could revoke them if a company did not fulfill its chartered purpose. Originally included in corporate charters, which were granted for a specific number of years, were their responsibilities to the communities they were in. Government authorities, representing the interests of the community, inspected the books and called companies to task for any misdeeds that violated their charter. But that is no more. Just as some of the Founding Fathers of our country feared, corporate power and money have eclipsed the power of our citizens to demand good citizenship. MegaMaws have now underhandedly gained the legal rights of individual citizens, to the detriment of our democratic ideals and values. Please see Thom Hartmann's book *Unequal Protection* and Marjorie Kelly's *The Divine Right of Capital* for the consequences to our democracy of unregulated MegaMaws, and how to bring them back under democratic control.

Cooperative Values

Although most small businesses in the Briarpatch Network were not structured as cooperatives, my own experience during that time was in the cooperatively owned and managed co-op store I've been telling you about. Consumer cooperatives and credit unions world-wide generally operate using the same set of values and principles.

A cooperative is an autonomous association of persons united voluntarily to meet their common economic, social, and cultural needs and aspirations through a jointly owned and democratically controlled enterprise. Cooperatives are based on the values of self-help, self-responsibility, democracy, equality, equity, and solidarity. In the tradition of the founders of the cooperative movement, which began in Rochdale, Lancashire, England, in the 1840s, cooperative members believe in the ethical values of honesty, openness, social responsibility, and caring for others. Here is a partial list of principles:

- Voluntary and open membership: Cooperatives are voluntary organizations, open to all persons able to use their services and willing to accept the responsibilities of membership, without gender, social, racial, political, or religious discrimination.

- Democratic member control: Cooperatives are democratic organizations controlled by their members, who actively participate in setting their policies and making decisions. Men and women serving as elected representatives are accountable to the membership. Members have equal voting rights — one member, one vote.

- Member economic participation: Members contribute equitably to and democratically control the capital of their cooperative.

- Autonomy and independence: Cooperatives are autonomous, self-help organizations controlled by their members.

- Concern for community: While focusing on member needs, cooperatives work for the sustainable development of their communities through policies accepted by their members.

The long, successful tradition of cooperative economics provides alternatives when business takes unfair advantage through monopolies and other unfair business practices. A community has ways to defend itself economically if it is disciplined, bands together, and cooperatively serves its own needs.

The Wisdom of Temperance

E. F. Schumacher was the leading business hero for many of us in the alternative small business community of the seventies. His book *Small Is Beautiful: Economics as If People Mattered* changed the way many people viewed the potential of business and its place in a sustainable society. Schumacher attacks corporate dominance, excessive materialism, and an economic system addicted to endless growth. Declaring one of the basic tenets of a sustainable economy, he writes, "A civilization built on renewable resources, such as the products of forestry and agriculture, is by this fact alone superior to one built on nonrenewable resources, such as oil, coal, metal, etc. This is because the former can last, while the latter cannot last. The former cooperates with nature, while the latter robs nature." He became adamantly opposed to the use of nuclear energy. The accumulation of large amounts of toxic substances, he claimed, "is a transgression against life itself."

Then, in his most famous essay, entitled "Buddhist Economics," he endorses a temperate view of work and economics: "Buddhist economics must be very different from the economics of modern materialism, since the Buddhist sees the essence of civilization not in a multiplication of wants but in the purification of human character. Character, at the same time, is formed primarily by a man's work. And work, properly conducted in conditions of human dignity and freedom, blesses those who do it and equally their products."

Money for Nothin'

We are led to believe that the American dream is to be a millionaire by age thirty and then go lie peacefully on the beach for the rest of our lives. We're told that a person will then have time to "give back" or "help the needy." I have yet to hear of a new lotto millionaire devoting his or her life to the common good, although there may be a few. But why would anyone want to lead a life of leisure? Is that goal personally fulfilling?

One good reason to leave the rat race to others and go to the beach is because most of our work has become meaningless. We've become slaves to the stuff and the lifestyles we've chosen. We imagine that it's better to leave it all than to continue in this state of enthrallment. But people generally want to contribute and want to live useful lives and earn their own way.

I've been lucky enough to have experienced, several times in my life, what I felt was a perfect match of my talents (meager as they might be), my values (as ill-formed and imprecise as they probably are), and my purpose in life (as dimly as I sometimes perceive it) with my chosen work. Cofounding and comanaging the Briarpatch Co-op was one of those experiences. My personality, idealism, and energies fit our community effort. Earlier, working with Cesar Chavez allowed me to apply technical skills I had developed for a worthy cause. And, much more recently, Diamond Organics calls upon the technical and managerial skills and experience I have developed over the years. That position, which I will explore in chapter 5, allowed me to hook up these personal resources with my primary passion for organic food and agriculture. I can recognize that perfect match simply by the way I feel. It begins with a peaceful feeling of usefulness to others and to the world I live in. Next comes the delightful feeling of working in concert with others who share my values. And after that is the ability to immerse myself fully, without hesitation or question, to the task at hand, and to draw endlessly from my creative energies, the energies that are always at the beck and call of those who are in the right place and time of their calling.

In each of those perfect matches, I made much less money than I did when those matches were less than perfect. As I've said, at the UFW, everyone, including Cesar, made the same income of room, board, and five dollars a week. At the Briarpatch Co-op, the pay was so low for the few paid staff that it was understood to be a temporary job with no future. At Diamond Organics, the margins for what are essentially commodities are so severely constrained by the marketplace that upper management, including the founders, are paid far below market salaries for the size of the company and the responsibilities required. One cannot survive long on labors of love, and depending on your stage of life, choices around work and income are often complicated and difficult. It helps to be in a community that supports alternative livelihoods, often found around college communities, giving more freedom to experiment and survive on lower incomes.

One of my favorite lines, from an old black-and-white movie, is "If you're so good, why aren't you poor?" A meaningful job most likely won't support a lavish lifestyle, although any job that doesn't support a decent living, whatever your own definition is, may not be worth the meaning it would give. A temperate approach is probably best.

Meaningful work comes alive
when temperance moderates thoughtless greed.
And that requires prudence....

prudence

[reclaiming the soul of business]

What is not worth doing, is not worth doing well.

— Abraham Maslow

It is not enough to be industrious; so are the ants. What are you industrious about?...

It is remarkable that there is little or nothing to be remembered written on the subject of getting a living; how to make getting a living not merely honest and honorable, but altogether inviting and glorious; for if getting a living is not so, then living is not....

— Henry David Thoreau

...the task of democracy is forever that of creation of a freer and more humane experience in which all share and to which all contribute.

— John Dewey

I wonder if you work in a small, cozy business, or a thriving medium-sized business, or a gigantic, transnational corporation? I love the small, beautiful, meaningful business that produces useful products and services along with a social purpose or mission. I've found that such a business, unless dominated by a despotic authoritarian jerk, need not worry about motivating employees because what most of us want out of a job is to be useful, contribute to the common good, and have fun.

Is your business like that? There are some businesses around like that, and they need good people like you. Unfortunately, they are not easy to find. Even more, our culture needs good people like you to create them and spin off other businesses like them. There are many people who want to support you and your business of purpose and who will choose your company over another that is just out to make a buck. Our culture and its investment class may have priorities that support much that is meaningless and superfluous. But there are niches that bring meaning and fulfillment, and as we and our culture progress, we can hope that a growing effort to find, even demand, meaningful work, which can only come with the demand for more quality and usefulness of products and services, will be met with new and creative companies that offer them. Maybe you'll start one.

Of course, you've got to get the basics right, like having a product or service that is needed, offering it at an affordable price, and being efficient, with empathetic customer service. But rules can be broken and risks taken. And you can't pretend you're something you're not by broadcasting all the good works you do and the huge percentage of your profit you give away when you aren't actually making a profit. Customers will smoke out your inauthenticity, email all their friends, and you'll walk around shaking your head at all the money you spent going to feel-good business conferences. The universe doesn't support you simply because you're "following your bliss." It does support damn hard and smart work with varying degrees of reward, both psychological and monetary.

The Way of the MegaMaw

Prudence is wisdom and sensibleness in practical matters like business. It counsels caution, foresight, and sound judgment. These are values that no longer seem honored, and terms that are now seldom used. Business today is all about big companies, fast companies, going for the gusto of get-rich-quick schemers and manipulators and immoderate dreamers.

In reality, we are a nation of small businesses. Only 1 percent of the corporations in America are larger than 500 employees. Only 4 percent of American corporations have more than $10 million in capitalization. Small businesses make up 99 percent of all American companies. But we know there's another side to this picture: The Fortune 1000 companies control about 70 percent of the American economy. Just two hundred corporations conduct almost one-third of the entire planet's economic activity and employ less than one-quarter of 1 percent of the world's workforce. Among the world's one hundred largest economies, over half are corporations, not countries. But the U.S. Bureau of Labor Statistics projects that 88 percent of all new job creation will come from small business.

In Japan and Germany, a typical CEO earns eight to ten times as much as a typical worker. In America the wage gap between a typical CEO and a typical worker grew from 40 to 1 in 1979 to 90 to 1 in 1995, and it now averages over 300 to 1. The outsourcing of service jobs to low-wage countries has further widened the pay gap between workers and their bosses. Currently, the pay gap between U.S. CEOs and American call center workers is 400 to 1, while the gap between U.S. CEOs and Indian call center workers is 3,348 to 1.

How does one best approach this injustice? Democratic unions are a crucial balance to the economic and political power of larger businesses. Trade and labor unions serve to dignify the lives and more fairly compensate the contributions of those who do the real work. But over the last thirty years, as unions have lost power and influence, the earnings of workers have stagnated or decreased. The unjust and unfair — no, I'm going to say it: the obscene and greedy — earnings demanded by irresponsible CEOs have skyrocketed because the balance of power has been destroyed. This is deep corruption at the heart of our democracy. It is theft by corporate leaders from their own workers, from their shareholders, and from the community.

Not all transnational corporations are bad. Big is not necessarily bad in itself. But the combination of legally designating corporations as persons, with all the rights of persons under our Constitution; deregulation that takes away democratic control; a Darwinian value system focused only on growing the bottom line; absentee ownership with no responsibility; and a business culture that cares nothing for democracy and everything for its own class has left us almost defenseless against businesses so huge and so powerful that our democracy is threatened and our entrepreneurial spirit often crushed by the demand to meet business plans requiring 30 and 40 percent annual profits and more. Outlaw MegaMaws are corporations that are aggressively unsustainable and socially irresponsible. They're the bully monopolists that bribe politicians and run roughshod over local communities. They're the deep pocket predators with voracious, never satisfied appetites for nature's ever shrinking bounty.

The unfortunate results of MegaMaw industrial agriculture and marketing are many. "Britain will this year export 111 million litres of milk and 47 million kilograms of butter," writes Helena Norberg-Hodge, director of the International Society of Ecology and Culture in Great Britain. "Simultaneously, we will import 173 million litres of milk and 49 million kilograms of butter. Apples will be flown 14,000 miles from New Zealand and green beans flown 4,000 miles from Kenya. We might wonder how these can possibly compete with local apples and beans: surely food produced locally should be cheaper. But it isn't. Generally speaking fresh local food is instead vastly more expensive than food from faraway. The main reason for this is government investments and subsidies." Our tax dollars at work against us.

What's wrong with that picture? A massive, wasteful amount of energy and economic resources are going to MegaMaws rather than to the farmers who grow the food. And yet we are told that the free market is the most efficient way to distribute goods. Surely there is a better way to coordinate markets and use precious, expensive energy resources than to ship in the same thing that was just shipped out.

As the lack of basic human values such as honesty and integrity has been revealed in big business scandals, the inevitable questions about how we've come to this and how to remedy it have been raised and agonized over. They are essentially questions about our values, about what should control our economic life: capital or people, money or democracy? Shouldn't we have "economics as if people matter"?

Following the revelations of corporate crime at the end of the nineties, several books have been published questioning the values practiced by corporations and the leaders who run them. In *The Corporation*, author Joel Bakan portrays basic corporate values as those of a psychopath: "purely self-interested, incapable of concern for others, amoral, and without conscience."

In *The Divine Right of Capital*, Marjorie Kelly, founder and editor of the magazine *Business Ethics*, writes: "After more than a decade of advocating corporate social responsibility and seeing its promise often thwarted, I've come to ask myself, *What is blocking change?* The answer is now obvious to me. It's the mandate to maximize returns for shareholders, which means serving the interests of wealth before all other interests. It is a systemwide mandate that cannot be overcome by individual companies. It is a legal mandate with which voluntary change can't compete. This mandate, quite simply, is a form of discrimination: wealth discrimination.... It is a form of entitlement out of place in a market economy." She goes on to decry rule by an "Economic Autocracy" and counsels that "we must return, in some measure, to the traditional liberties that were America's founding ideals: the liberty of states to control corporations, the liberty of casting a vote that has substance, the liberty of enjoying the fruits of our own labor, and the liberty of individuals to enjoy equality under the law. These are liberties that corporations and the wealthy have usurped, and they are liberties we can rightfully reclaim."

In *Unequal Protection*, Thom Hartmann documents how Thomas Jefferson unsuccessfully tried to include in the Bill of Rights the protection of humans from "commercial monopolies." From this Hartmann argues that depending on legal reform is insufficient. He writes: "[W]hat is needed is a foundational change in the definition of the relationship between living human beings and the nonliving legal fictions we call corporations. Only when corporations are again legally subordinate to those who authorized them — humans, and the governments representing them — will true change be possible." This will require "a grassroots movement in communities all across America and the world to undo corporate personhood, leading to changes in the definitions of the word 'person.'

"History tells us that when corporate power is unrestrained, and corporations grow so large that the largest among them come to control and then stifle the marketplace, the result is the corruption of democracy followed by economic collapse... and we're seeing this writ large today, with the same consequences. Democracy is under assault and America is becoming impoverished."

Early in my career, before I understood anything about what social conscience was, I worked for a MegaMaw defense contractor. I was well trained in the technical aspects of my job. I could efficiently punch the buttons, mount and dismount the computer tapes, print the reports, and track the various operations from start to finish quickly and efficiently, but I didn't have a clue about what the reports meant or what the company actually did. For security purposes, most of the manufacturing area was off-limits to me, and I honestly didn't really care what the company did. I knew it made helicopters somewhere for the armed services, but it was a huge company and I was in a small division of it.

There was no connection between the work I did and the ultimate output of the company. I was informed of things on a "need to know basis," and there wasn't anything else I needed to know other than how to do my rote job. Someone, somewhere knew, but who and where and why, I knew not.

Feeding the Beast

To get a close-up view of the modern MegaMaw, we can visit the MegaMaw plantation and peer through the fences at some examples of what roams in its metaphorical pastures. What you see is *not* what you get.

You're looking at the corporate equivalent of Jurassic Park. You see that large reptilian creature contentedly grazing in pastureland? It's a MegaMaw, a machine. Inside it are human beings (called Insiders and Programmers) with computers that manipulate the huge beast so that it appears to be a real, living animal.

These creatures are made up from somebody's imagination. Never forget for a second that they are programmed to do these three things only — feed, grow, and perform whatever their Insiders and Programmers demand of them. To do their Insider's bidding they take time out from eating and growing to do "piecework" with their tiny hands. The little ones, MiniMaws, are programmed to put things together, millions of useless plastic knickknacks and paddiwacks, and assemble packaged plant sticks the Insiders insist they make so the Masters can smoke them and kill themselves. Very strange fruits in this MegaMaw land.

As they continue to grow larger, these creatures become Mega-Maws and take on larger projects, such as assembling bombs and missiles. They can do many things well as they keep eating and growing. In the background you will notice Programmers building taller and stouter fencing for the growing beasts, but don't kid yourself. Many have escaped their pens with dire consequences, so be on full alert at all times. Now and then a beast will pause, swing its massive head to and fro, and eyeball other MegaMaws and MiniMaws around it. Then suddenly, without warning, it'll chow down on one of its own, causing the others to eat faster and faster, trying to get too massive to be consumed themselves.

MegaMaw Scat

The term "scat" comes from a MegaMaw tendency that Insiders call the "drop and scat." Although the MegaMaw creatures are huge and scary looking, they are quite shy about the waste they create, slinking around in the dead of night looking for a place to — well, how to put it delicately — uh, drop their load. Waterways are favored, but they are also known to dig deep trenches to avoid detection. They may use discarded barrels to bury their excrement in. Their Bean Counters use phrases like "externalizing costs" and "outsourcing waste"; Insiders call it "shit canning."

Even though this secretive waste disposal is against the original programming that created MegaMaw behavior, rogue Programmers have apparently hacked in and created the "worms" that cause the discharge, because the behavior is always a mystery to the Insiders and Programmers when it is discovered. They have no idea how it could have happened, and they maintain that it must have been some other MegaMaw that created the stink, not their own.

Some think that the cause is an error in the original program that has not yet been found and debugged. Who knows? But then, who pays? Usually we all do because no one takes responsibility, or the offending MegaMaw cannot be found, or the MegaMaw has been devoured by a larger MegaMaw who takes no responsibility for what the other one did.

This becomes a real problem when a MegaMaw arrives in your neighborhood. Say a new neighbor buys up several homes next to yours, demolishes them, and builds a huge new thirty-room mansion. It turns out he's an Insider and he has a MiniMaw (about a ten-tonner) roaming his back yard. The week after he moves in, you wander out your back door and discover that the huge creature has knocked down your fence and pooped your lawn. Incredulous, you take a brisk ten-minute walk across *his* lawn and ring the doorbell (which continues to echo throughout the mansion's corridors for several minutes). The new neighbor eventually opens the door. A short man about four feet tall and four feet wide, he introduces himself as Mr. P. Crat. As he talks, his hands are in constant motion, touching his pockets and stomach and chest as if to keep making sure he's still there ... and he'll adjust his glasses over and over, and clear his throat every three or four words, and look back over his shoulder ... all in an unending battle to keep his act together.

You tell him that something knocked over the fence last night and pooped your lawn. It's so massive and stinks so badly you're thinking it should be designated a Superfund site. He says, "Oh, yeah? Sorry about that, but could you help me out a bit? I'm a bottom-line kind of guy, and when I found out just how expensive waste removal is around here, especially with all the waste my little guy produces, I decided it would impact my monthly budget way too much, so I figured I could 'off-load' that expense onto the neighborhood in general. I hope you understand. Maybe you could share the expense by taking up a monthly collection around the neighborhood. I just don't have the time. Do you mind?"

Trying to keep from going ballistic, you ask him what planet he came from. He smiles and shrugs his shoulders, saying that he just moved into town from a large piece of property in the country where he never had to deal with going to the dump. He could simply have it burned in a barrel or dumped in the creek or buried in the ground or hauled to an on-site "lagoon" ... and that he wasn't about to start paying fees for removal mandated by some small-time local government regulatory agency. "That's just not the way you do things in a free country," he explains, getting more and more flustered, "and last time I looked it still was a *free country*. We let the market decide and, damn it, I'm just not in the market right now for solid waste service. Besides," he continues, suddenly calm and looking you straight in the eye, "I need the money for research and development, we're working on a very important product that will be of tremendous benefit to humankind."

Apoplectic at such clueless, selfish, unneighborly behavior, you tell him that under no circumstances is that to ever happen again or you'll have the police department driving up his circular driveway.

"Oh," he says, "bring 'em on! The worst they'll do is fine me ten bucks and be on their way. Look, I'm really a valuable addition to this neighborhood. I'm going to hire kids around here to mow my lawn and wash my cars and babysit my dogs and take care of other chores around here that I just cannot be bothered with. Tell you what. The haul fee would cost me thousands a month, so what if I give you ten bucks right now and you can run along and round up the rest of the monthly bill from the other neighbors and start paying for it as a community service. If someone finds out about the ten bucks we'll just say there is no connection whatsoever between it and the fees that the other neighbors are paying every month. We'll say that it was just a friendly donation with no strings attached, and that you're simply interested in keeping the neighborhood neat and tidy and everyone needs to pitch in. And by the way, would you like to take a ride with me in one of my limos to visit my church next Sunday?"

This scenario presents one of the great breakdowns of our economic system. It's called "externalizing costs" in current business parlance, and it means making someone else besides the manufacturer or the consumer pay a cost involved in making a product. Someone has to pay for the health-care costs created by air pollution, but it sure isn't the coal plants or car drivers. It's all of us, whether we had anything directly to do with it or not. In values terms, externalizing costs could be called "crass irresponsibility." We experience its effects by living downstream and drinking the effluent dumped by a chemical company, and by living downwind and breathing the radioactive elements from nuclear plants.

Why is there mercury in the fish we eat, or rather, that we can't eat because they are unsafe now? Why are there particulates that cause asthma and cancer in the air our children breathe? Is it because we don't have the technology to stop the pollution? No. Shouldn't it then be against the law? Yes, it is against the law. Why are they allowed to break the law? Because it's cheaper to pay politicians not to enforce the law than it is to clean up *their* waste before it becomes *our* waste. Price is important.

By not being responsible for cleaning up their own wastes, MegaMaws internalize their profits while externalizing their costs, and this internalizes their wastes in our bodies. When a company lowers its costs, its investors can make more money, and its CEO, who pays off the politicians with campaign donations and other bribes, can increase the share price of his company's (and his own) stock while making a higher salary. If he gets caught because he neglected to pay off someone, the light fine his company will pay is far less than the cost of obeying the law. For them it's a win-win-win-win. The company wins, the CEO wins, the investors win, the politicians win. The rest of us lose.

Well, some of us lose. Over half of the families in America are now investors in the stock market, playing the same game trying to get ahead, to increase our own capital for college money or for retirement, making it very difficult to point fingers and blame the "bad guys."

What happens when a publicly traded MegaMaw CEO decides to pay attention to the negative effects that a company is having on the local community and wants to spend money on cleaning up and reducing pollution? Costs go up, profits go down, and the ever-lurking corporate raiders spot an opportunity for more profits — profits that are being lost to someone's good conscience. The company is "put into play." The board must make decisions in the best interests of shareholders, so it is sold, the CEO ousted, pieces of the company sold off or shrunk down, thousands of jobs lost, and a community devastated.

And say you work for one of these bad-neighbor MegaMaw

scofflaws that have not been properly potty-trained. There is better work, work that will be good for your soul. There are now websites, like IdealsWork.com, that track the behavior of companies. Employees can use the Internet to check on their own company's behavior and then decide whether to buck the system and work to change things internally, or leave for greener pastures. *Business Ethics* magazine annually ranks the one hundred best companies to work for. You may need to find one that is smaller, privately held, and less beholden to the unethical public stock markets.

The Way We Work Now

I've long been searching for ways to apply good values in business, to work with socially responsible businesses, and to experience workplaces that are exuberant with mission and fun — to go even beyond being socially responsible as a business to being socially *active* as a business. Social activism is a big no-no to big-time, big-business gurus such as economist Milton Friedman and Peter Drucker. Friedman believes that there is but one social responsibility for corporate executives: they must make as much money as possible for their shareholders. Indeed, choosing social and environmental goals over profits, for Friedman, is immoral. He goes further in stating that there is only one way that corporate social responsibility can be tolerated, and that is when it is insincere, used only to maximize shareholders' wealth by falsely claiming social responsibility rather than actually practicing it. Drucker has stated: "If you find an executive who wants to take on social responsibilities, fire him. Fast."

Friedman and Drucker, our greatest living economist and our greatest living business guru, as designated by the popular business press, have turned virtues and values into their opposites, making morality immoral, and hypocrisy a virtue. These immoral imperatives are also required by the law that governs our modern corporations — the only line is the bottom line, the profit line. This allows corporations to ignore the impact of their decisions on people and communities. CEOs must meditate unwaveringly on that line. It must climb, eternally and forever, people and communities and environments be damned.

Today's News: Externalizing Costs, Outsourcing Grief and Sorrow

A random walk through the consequences of values-free corporate behavior yields the following:

- Curaçao citizens organize a campaign called the Humane Care Foundation to hold Shell Oil liable for the massive damage that it has inflicted on the community, including significant toxic damage that affects more than 5,500 children.

- Bayer's GE [genetically engineered] crop herbicide Finale, based on the active ingredient glufosinate-ammonium, is widely used in the United States and has been found to cause brain damage. Adult consumers are most likely to be exposed to residues of glufosinate in potatoes.

- Infant death rates near five U.S. nuclear plants drop immediately and dramatically after the reactors are closed.

- An unprecedented joint statement issued by the leading scientific academies of the world has called on the G8 governments to take urgent action to avert a global catastrophe caused by climate change.

- Fifty-five thousand people have likely died from taking the painkiller Vioxx, even though Merck, the pharmaceutical company that developed it, knew of the drug's adverse effect four years before taking it off the market. Sales have been worth $2.5 billion a year.

- More than 5 million children alive today will die prematurely from smoking-related illnesses.

- Nearly 95 percent of corporations now pay less than 5 percent of their income in taxes.

Corporations as People

The U.S. Constitution never mentions corporations, but some of our founders foresaw that corporations could become the uncontrollable, heartless beasts that many have become when they grow too large and powerful and monopolistic. It was MegaMaw tea that was dumped in Boston harbor by the Sons of Liberty protesting the imperialism of British trading companies. Jefferson, Madison, and others knew that even the MegaMaws of their day were antidemocratic entities that could amass more money than the public could muster and could absolve themselves personally from responsibility for any damage done. Today's MegaMaw structure allows the owners to reap the profits of the company's activity, while they themselves, and their personal assets, are protected from any responsibility for damage they do. As Jim Hightower says, "Corporations can live forever, don't need clean air and water to live, can't be put in jail, have no moral restraints of their own, and no other goal but to keep growing and keep the profits flowing."

In the 1800s, for a corporation to get a state charter, it had to have a public purpose, such as building educational institutions, and if it failed in its public purpose it would lose its charter and be dissolved. It could not purchase or merge with another corporation and could grow only to a predesignated size. A charter usually expired after fifteen or twenty years, requiring renewal and examination of its public contribution and continuing need to exist. It also had to treat farmers and other businesses and suppliers fairly and responsibly and could never contribute to politicians, or engage in lobbying and politics. Democracy was for one person, one vote citizenry.

If prudent citizenship is to be sensible and to use sound judgment, MegaMaws have to be identified as imprudent citizens, unworthy of the freedoms they have accumulated under the guise of being legal humans. Those freedoms must now be withdrawn by a prudent, democratic citizenry that regulates corporations to either cease business or responsibly keep their garbage to themselves: the mercury spewing from their smokestacks; the poisons spewing from their chemical plants; the genetically modified organisms polluting our food; the shit and piss from the factories that "process" horribly mistreated animals.

A good first step would be political reform. As Teddy Roosevelt advised, "There can be no effective control of corporations while their political activity remains." A 1907 law makes it illegal for politicians to accept money from corporations. Of course, almost one hundred years later, it is not enforced. Nor is the Sherman Antitrust Act of 1890. Real campaign finance reform should be one of our most pressing priorities, a reform that would spur many others.

Democracy, and the middle class, will not survive the Mega-Maws running amuck on our planet, but we can rein them in. They were dealt with effectively by the Boston Tea Party, again by the Grange movement in the late 1800s, and yet again by the labor movement of the 1930s. Each time Americans came back and reassumed their democratic rights. We are called upon yet again to assert the freedoms and rights that are under determined assault from within. Democracy will always eventually prevail. Hope rests in the strength of our values that operate for the common good.

Absentee Ownership

Public stock ownership, where ownership has no connection to a company other than to ensure that the dollar value of ownership increases more than, and in competition with, the dollar value of other public companies, fundamentally violates traditional wisdom, summed up by the Christian scripture "The *love* of money is the root (and also the route) of all evil." It is immoral to increase the value of money without any connection whatever to *how* it is increased and the *effect* of its increase on others. Often to disastrous effect, the moment investors think a company is not going to increase their wealth as fast as some other company whose stock is traded on the exchange, the investment is withdrawn and reinvested in a nanosecond. These decisions are made by the billions daily, and have no relation to what is moral or immoral, right or wrong, good or bad.

Quite simply, when investors insist that a company continue to increase its quarterly profits regardless of morality, many companies and many CEOs will act immorally to increase profits. It is their job. If they are making three hundred times the average pay of their workers, they've been bought off to act immorally at the behest of others. They are not three hundred times smarter, or three hundred times more efficient. They are being reimbursed for the toll it takes on their soul.

The downside of greed is summed up by George Bernard Shaw's rejoinder: "Lack of money is the root of all evil." Nature wants balance. As greed escalates, hunger increases. The more millionaires, the more soup kitchens. Some would have us believe that poverty is a result of laxity on the part of those who are poor, rather than placing responsibility at the doorstep of those who justify their greed by claiming that the only moral responsibility of a business is to maximize its owner's wealth.

Greed has always been identified as one of the social sins by traditional wisdom. It results in injustice. Gandhi listed what he called the Seven Deadly Social Sins, those he considered spiritually damaging:

- politics without principle
- wealth without work
- commerce without morality
- pleasure without conscience
- education without character

- science without humanity
- worship without sacrifice

If we consider greed to be worship of money, then public stock, solely to increase its value without regard to its impact on our neighbors, is to directly or indirectly participate in all seven of Gandhi's social sins.

Theodore Roszak, in his introduction to E. F. Schumacher's *Small Is Beautiful*, wrote: "[W]e need a nobler economics that is not afraid to discuss spirit and conscience, moral purpose and the meaning of life...." In this, the richest country ever to exist on Earth, if millions of hardworking, responsible citizens can't find meaningful jobs that pay a living wage, allowing them the time and money to pursue spiritual and material happiness, then there is something wrong in our democracy. If they cannot choose work that fits their intelligence and skills and meets their need to be useful and contribute, then there is something wrong with our culture. If they cannot afford to get sick, then there is something wrong with our economic system. If they have given up having any effect on their democratic representatives because the rich and powerful have bought and paid for their attention and decisions, then there is something wrong with our politics.

Business by the Golden Rule

Now the good news — the way things *could* be. There are many ways to introduce more democracy into the workplace. But it always has to start with honesty and openness. Our business culture has become so competitive and cutthroat that fear rules over common sense. We set policies and rules to cover any negative contingency or possibility, and in the process we shut down the creativity, open communication, and trust necessary for a democratic workplace. It is certainly necessary to protect trade secrets and product development, but I wonder how much secrecy is really about protecting turf and butts, and how much more competitive a company would be by simply throwing away the secrecy codes and opening up the company to a lot more air and sunshine.

No One in Charge?

...or everyone in charge? Semco Incorporated of São Paulo, Brazil, is an industrial pump manufacturer that grew into a conglomerate of property management, professional services, and high-tech spin-offs. It has grown from $35 million in annual revenue to $212 million in the last six years. Even with more than three thousand employees, its workforce has virtually no turnover. CEO Ricardo Semler encourages his employees to play hooky and tells them not to bother with growth plans. Employees choose their own salaries, pick their own managers, and set their own hours, and have no job titles. The company has no mission statement, rule book, or written policies. There is no organization chart, no job titles, no HR department. Subordinates choose their managers and decide their own pay. Meeting attendance is voluntary, and board meetings leave two seats open for the first two employees who show up. Salary and other company financial information is open to the public. Semco proves that a company that puts employee freedom and happiness ahead of corporate goals and decides things democratically instead of hierarchically can achieve profit, sustainability, and growth that far exceed the competition's. You may think that this just shows how Brazilians' love of life is more powerful than their love of traditional management practices, but I believe it really shows that when a company actually practices trust and treats employees as adults, the result is cooperation, self-management, and self-discipline. If we would be more creative and experimental with management practices, I think we would find the happiness of employees and their sense of meaning rise dramatically.

In his book *The Seven-Day Weekend*, Semler writes: "When visitors learn that our economic success requires replacing control and structure with democracy in the workplace — well, often those starry-eyed visiting executives go home with second thoughts and never get around to making it happen in their workplaces.... Why do organizations and their leaders cling to a rigid form of command and control that is at odds with the values of personal freedom that they cherish?... If employees can come in anytime, work anywhere, and take sole charge of their hours, how can they be controlled? At Semco, managers are concerned with the essence of what employees do for the company, nothing more.... So it all comes back to that hardest of all reforms, relinquishing control, and giving it up happily.

"On-the-job democracy isn't just a lofty concept but a better, more profitable way to do things. We all demand democracy in every other aspect of our lives and culture. People are considered adults in their private lives, at the bank, at their children's schools, with family and among friends — so why are they suddenly treated like adolescents at work? Why can't workers be involved in choosing their own leaders? Why shouldn't they manage themselves? Why can't they speak up — challenge, question, share information openly?"

Here are some more inspiring details from *The Semco Survival Manual:*

ORGANIZATION CHART – *Semco doesn't use a formal organization chart. Only the respect of the led creates a leader. When it is absolutely necessary to sketch the structure of some part of the company, we always do it in pencil, and dispense with it as soon as possible.*

HIRING – *When people are hired or promoted, the others in that unit have the opportunity to interview and evaluate the candidates before any decision is made.*

WORKING HOURS – *Semco has flexible working hours, and the responsibility for setting and keeping track of them rests with each employee. People* work at different speeds and differ in their performance depending on the time of day. Semco does its best to adapt to each person's desires and needs.

WORKING ENVIRONMENT — *We want all our people to feel free to change and adapt their working area as they please. Painting walls or machines, adding plants or decorating the space around you is up to you. The company has no rules about this, and doesn't want to have any. Change the area around you according to your tastes and desires and those of the people who work with you.*

UNIONS — *Unions are an important form of worker protection. At Semco, workers are free to unionize and the persecution of those connected with unions is absolutely forbidden. Unions and the company don't always agree or even get along, but we insist that there is always mutual respect and dialog.*

STRIKES — *Strikes are considered normal. They are part and parcel of democracy. No one is persecuted for participating in strikes, as long as they represent what the people of the company think and feel. The workers' assemblies are sovereign in this respect. Absence at work for reasons of strike is considered as normal absenteeism, without further consequences or punishments.*

PARTICIPATION — *Our philosophy is built on participation and involvement. Don't settle down. Give opinions, seek opportunities and advancement, always say what you think. Don't just be one more person in the company. Your opinion is always interesting, even if no one asked you for it. Get in touch with the factory committees, and participate in elections. Make your voice count.*

EVALUATION BY SUBORDINATES — *Twice a year you will receive a questionnaire to fill out that enables you to say what you think of your boss. Be very frank and honest, not just on the form but also in the discussion that follows.*

AUTHORITY — *Many positions at Semco carry with them hierarchical authority. But efforts to pressure subordinates or cause them to work out of fear or insecurity, or that show any type of disrespect, are considered an unacceptable use of authority and will not be tolerated.*

CLOTHING AND APPEARANCE – *Neither has any importance at Semco. A person's appearance is not a factor in hiring or promotion. Everyone knows what he or she likes or needs to wear. Feel at ease — wear only your common sense.*

INFORMALITY – *Promoting a birthday party at the end of the workday, barging into meetings where you were not invited, or using nicknames are all part of our culture. Don't be shy or stick to formalities.*

We spend many millions of dollars annually in business schools across the country; on business books selling the latest, greatest system of management; and on business gurus, who, like charismatic evangelists selling their branded religion, jump up and down in conferences trying to rev up our enthusiasm for new company missions. Yet research and experience repeatedly show that when employees are given responsibility, treated like adults, fairly rewarded with company stock, and allowed to democratically participate in their company's decisions, you simply can't keep a company from thriving. We are stuck in our top-down mind-set when what is desperately needed is bottom-up democracy. Open, democratic inclusion brings passion and meaning to earning our daily bread.

Human Values

Cheap food is not healthy food. Making and buying better quality food and goods rebound in favor of the workers because it makes it possible for them to take pride in, and get paid for, quality. Dousing strawberries with pesticides produces big, beautiful, poor-quality, tasteless, poisoned fruit. Strawberries grown with hand labor (but *not* backbreaking exploitation) and attention to detail produce *better* quality, tasty, healthy fruit that is worth more in the market and thus affords a better profit for the farmer and a better wage for the workers.

I recently heard a very passionate and articulate farmer arguing that the unionization of small farms, though good for farmworkers, would bankrupt him. He spoke about his love of "*my* workers" and how well he treated "*my* crew." Treating anyone as a belonging is disrespectful of them and their independent freedom. It's an unfortunate paternalistic language long associated with farm labor, and the worst part is that it correctly describes the way things really work on many farms, in spite of good, openhearted intentions. This farmer, like many others, was missing the point.

Jim Cochran is an organic strawberry farmer on the central coast of California. How does he love and honor the people he works with? Does he act the typical farm boss, maybe like a benevolent dictator, but a dictator nonetheless? Does he run things *his* way? Or is he more "democratic," meaning he *allows* democratic input and *lets* his workers make decisions? He's a small businessman with his whole life's work at stake with every decision. Why would he want to allow anyone else any power whatsoever over crucial decisions that could waste a lifetime of heart-and-soul investment? *He's* the person who sweated and strained to bring this business to life. It's *his* life and *his* money. No one else should ever have the right to decide anything really important, should they?

For me, this comes full circle. Since my years of working with Cesar Chavez, I've been involved with many businesspeople who genuinely care for their employees and take good care of them. But I have never worked with any that would allow a union to organize. True, these businesses were mostly made up of white-collar workers, who seldom organize into unions; the companies were small startups, and they were often generous with stock options for professionals. None of them would have been considered large enough to organize a union in, or were part of an identifiable industry that unions were targeting. Still, some employed blue-collar labor, and though they practiced enlightened management, the idea of their workers joining a union was either not considered or would have been actively opposed. Many of us, including myself, have believed that enlightened management practices precluded the need for unions. "Why would they want or need to do that? We treat them so well!" This, of course, echoes the Southern plantation owner's attitude toward emancipation. One of the glaring omissions in the organic food movement is that certification of organic foods includes meticulously detailed standards for how the soil is treated, but not one word about how workers should be. Even Whole Foods, a paragon of New Age management techniques and widely heralded as a progressive company, is virulently antiunion.

Jim Cochran thinks and acts differently. The dignity of farm labor was a founding principle of his company, Swanton Berry Farm. Jim wanted to present his customers with good food that was not produced at the expense of the workers' health or dignity. Jim reasoned: "What would be the point of farming organically, respecting the Earth and the environment, if the workers were underpaid, overworked, and treated without respect?" Offering a chemical-free work environment is an important step, but simply carrying the "organic" label does not address issues such as pay and benefits. There are many more factors that go into creating a good work environment.

Swanton Berry Farm was the first strawberry farm (and the first organic farm) in the United States to sign a contract with the United Farm Workers Union. And it didn't happen because of labor unrest, strikes, or picket lines. Jim invited the union into his farm because he cared.

The unionization of Swanton employees gives them the ability to sit across the table with management and discuss issues as equals — copartners in their joint effort to produce the best strawberries available anywhere. A grievance procedure sets the structure for resolving differences. (Interestingly, in the seven years since the farm was unionized, no grievances have been filed.) The last step is binding arbitration. All of this gives the workers the best pay scale in the industry, a medical plan, a retirement plan, and vacation and holiday pay.

This package naturally raises the cost of strawberries, but Jim feels that their customers will be happy to pay more knowing that the workforce is treated fairly and the food is produced under the best working conditions. The farm pays at an hourly rate rather than a piece rate, so that people don't scramble so fast that they do permanent damage to their bodies in the rush to make a few more dollars in the day. The farm gives unlimited time off for employees to attend to their children's needs. During any given day, one or two or three employees will leave for a while to take care of some family business. Doing the same task over and over again is not only boring, but it can also be physically harmful. But since Swanton grows a number of different crops, workers can enjoy some variety in work tasks during a given week. A typical workweek will involve strawberry picking, weeding, and harvesting vegetables.

"We also try to have a good time!" Jim says. "While farmwork is hard work, it is made easier by good companionship and good humor." He recognizes the fact that everything they do springs from work done in the field. They involve as many employees as possible in the decision-making process and share as much information as possible with them. Thus farmwork at Swanton Berry Farm is an intellectual as well as a physical process. "We depend on the ideas and observations of all employees. It takes a bit longer to do things when you ask several opinions about what should be done next, but in the end, we make better decisions.... We treat all of our employees as professionals, not cogs in a 'food machine'."

Well, you may say, that does take a lot of courage, but it hardly seems prudent. His costs and prices must have gone up substantially. Yes, they did. And how did Jim deal with that? "I decided that it was *my* responsibility to work with our customers and consumers to explain why our prices were going up and how important it was that they support workers living a decent life. We also display the union logo prominently on our boxes so everyone knows that our workers are represented democratically."

The next step is already under way at Swanton Berry Farm of giving workers increasing ownership of the business that they are helping to build. (For more information about the farm, go to www.swanton berryfarm.com.)

This all started when Cesar Chavez — a man small in stature, the color of the earth, and so shy that at his first neighborhood organizing meeting when everyone had gathered and was waiting to get started, someone finally had to ask, "Where's the organizer?" — demanded equality and dignity for himself, his family, and his neighbors, and changed the world for the better. It has been ultimately fulfilled by a farmer who cares and believes in decent human values as a way to live and work.

Cooperative Business

The Mondragón cooperatives of Spain combine credit unions and service cooperatives such as grocery stores with industrial manufacturing cooperatives, research centers, and a university — all as one integrated unit. As a cooperative corporation, they are "an association of persons rather than an association of capital." That means one person, one vote rather than votes apportioned to capital invested. It also means that the individual workers own and control the company they work in. They are the largest worker-owned cooperative in the world, doing many billions of dollars in sales. They own and operate thousands of supermarkets, a travel agency with hundreds of units, and gas stations. They also manufacture automotive parts, domestic appliances, bicycles, and bus bodies.

The Mondragón cooperative model can be compared to the MegaMaw structure as follows:

- Owner-workers are valued as people. Management professionalism, product excellence, and customer satisfaction matter more than the rapid growth of profits.

- Owner-workers participate in management, with salary differences limited to a three-to-one ratio, rather than just being used at the whim of a grossly overpaid management class.

- The social contract commits everyone involved to the development of the business, with member-owner security and partnership with capital, rather than confrontation between labor and capital.

- Profits and losses are shared among all proportionally, rather than profits being internalized and costs being externalized irresponsibly.

Mondragón's Community Bank, a credit union that serves as the core of its financial system, is owned and controlled by the member-owners of the cooperative. Without their own banking system, the cooperative would have failed. The bank invests in the development of new enterprises under the motto "Savings or Suitcases," meaning members can either invest in their own community or watch their money leave their community to work elsewhere and enrich others. The cooperatives also operate their own social security facility, which provides unemployment insurance, medical services, and medical insurance.

The Mondragón consumer cooperative grocery chain, with 264 stores, is run by a general assembly composed of an equal number of consumer-members and worker-members. The assembly elects a board that is similarly balanced, with six employees and six consumer-members, with a chairperson who is always a consumer.

Mondragón principles include (1) openness to all, regardless of ethnic background, religion, political beliefs, or gender; (2) the equality of all owner-workers and democratic control on the basis of one member, one vote; (3) the recognition of labor as the most essential, transformative factor of society and the renunciation of wage labor in favor of the full power of owner-workers to control the co-ops and distribute surpluses; (4) a definition of capital as accumulated labor, necessary for development and savings, with a limited return paid on that capital; (5) cooperation, defined as the development of the individual *with* others, not *against* others, to self-manage (managers are elected by the workers) and develop training and skills; and (6) wages that are comparable to prevailing local standards.

According to Don José María Arizmendiarrieta, the founder of Mondragón: "Cooperation is the authentic integration of people in the economic and social process that shapes a new social order; the cooperators must make this objective extend to all those that hunger and thirst for justice in the working world."

Greg MacLeod, author of *From Mondragon to America*, writes: "The Cooperative Corporation itself is a moral entity having responsibility at three levels: (1) towards the individual employees, (2) towards the cooperative corporations which make up the Mondragon family, and (3) towards the general society of which it is the basic unit. As a microcosm of the general society, the enterprise must practice all the virtues demanded of the total society such as respect for the members, personal development and educational programs, social security and distributive justice."

This successful alternative to the classic, top-down corporate MegaMaw allows thinking outside the box store. Bottom-up democracy works and is the next step in bringing meaning into our work as well as our politics. Some of our politicians love to constantly spout off about bringing democracy to other nations, even if it takes our bombers and infantry to preemptively force it on them. Politicians who love democracy should not stop with politics. Let's take them at their word and ask them to help us complete the American revolution by bringing democracy into our workplaces and our economics. True democracy in our workplaces and in our economics is a much better way to bring democracy to our neighbors: with working examples.

Slow Company

I've had the privilege to serve on the board of directors and work on and off as a marketing consultant at Diamond Organics. Located on Highway 1 in Moss Landing, California, where it is neighbor to the largest concentration of organic farms in the country, Diamond Organics ships organic vegetables, fruits, meat, cheese, bulk grains, and other foods directly to consumers across the United States via FedEx and UPS. Our customers order by phone or website, we ship their order by the end of the day, and they receive it the following day. Thus they receive the freshest organic food money can buy.

For some customers, Diamond Organics products are a luxury; for others, they are a godsend. Most consumers on the East Coast get their produce trucked in from the West Coast many days old, and since the nutritional value of fresh food decays over time, its taste and value for one's health are also lowered. We have customers who because of ill health have been prescribed a strict organic food diet by their doctors, and we're their only source. (Of course, eating organically is not only a good treatment, it is also a very effective preventive measure.)

Diamond Organics is a mom-and-pop business founded by Jasch and Kathleen Hamilton. With current annual sales of over $3 million, it has grown slowly but steadily for the past fourteen years and has a devoted customer base across the country. I will usually come in for a few months to help out with marketing and operations, as well as wherever else I'm needed. Things get busy every Monday, and prior to the holidays, and then it's pedal to the metal, all hands on deck. We all take orders on the phone and pick produce for the packers.

Shipping fresh by air is expensive and environmentally incorrect. Yet the most efficient delivery system we have in this country is via UPS and FedEx. Distributing products to neighborhoods by truck is much more efficient, economical, and environmentally less damaging than having a member of each household drive a car to a supermarket. Most efficient of all, of course, is growing your own in the backyard, or having it delivered directly from a local farm to a distribution point. The dream of Diamond Organics is to have several distribution points around the country so we can purchase from local farms during the summer, shipping from California only during the winter months when local produce is unavailable.

Company cofounder Jasch Hamilton has an interesting story. He apparently began developing a slow-growth brain tumor several years ago, but he discovered it only about four years ago when he began having seizures. The worst one came while he was driving with his son and a friend. As he felt the seizure coming on, he pulled off the road, but as he tried desperately to jam the transmission into park, the grand mal seizure struck, forcing his foot onto the gas pedal. The car shot across the road and straight into a building. Fortunately, the air bags saved everyone from injury, but Jasch lost his license and could no longer drive.

Refusing radiation treatment and any sampling the doctors wanted to do by drilling into his brain, Jasch went on a strict macrobiotic diet. But brain scans showed that the tumor was continuing its slow growth. Jasch gave up that diet and decided he was just going to live well, take some vitamins and medicine, and make every hour count. He read that medicinal properties in green tea had been shown to stop tumor growth, so he visited China and began importing and drinking the best organic green tea he could find. He also began taking hot baths at Esalen, a couple of hours south of us, in Big Sur. He would continually question how others could waste their time on movies and other entertainment when life was so short.

After a few months, not thinking anything much had changed, he went in for another brain scan. This one showed a miraculous shrinkage. Dumbfounded, his doctor said, "This just doesn't happen." Jasch has had no more seizures, has his driver's license back, and he's watching movies again, though infrequently.

Here's what I want to tell you about Diamond Organics.

Remember the miserable, alienated guy in chapter 4 who worked at the company where "the phone does not stop"? Sometimes it doesn't stop at Diamond Organics either, but it doesn't make anyone miserable. We all jump in and take our turn, and we love the interaction with customers. What's the difference? For one, we have many customers who order every week and have a fond relationship with the company because of how fully their needs are being met. And we who provide service to them feel great about what we sell and why we sell it. It's good, fresh, healthy food, with a spirit of genuine service and camaraderie. And there's no strict dividing line between those who only manage and those who only do the work.

The other thing I want tell you about Diamond Organics is its grassroots way of funding the business. They raise capital directly from their customers using direct public offerings (DPOs). To date, they have raised over $1 million from 150 customers, and with that they have been able to finance their growth and build a new building. The share price has escalated steadily to its current price of $8 a share. DPOs have been used successfully over the past few years to finance other small, growing companies and are an especially good alternative for small companies who are doing good work in the world.

The difference between a DPO and a public offering on the stock exchange is that with a DPO, a community is investing in a service to itself, with the sales of shares being marketed directly to the customers of the service. Although anyone can invest, the crucial difference lies in the prior relationship of those serving and being served. Customers are capitalizing a community service they care about because of its service to them, rather than investing in the stock market, where almost the only consideration is return on investment.

When Big Turns Beautiful

It has been disheartening to watch the values of the triple bottom line (profitability, environmental sustainability, and social responsibility) being applied by huge, unsustainable, socially irresponsible multinationals to *greenwash* their image in full-page magazine ads. But here and there are companies who've taken their efforts seriously and are leading the way in converting worldwide operations into a steady, gradual conversion to sustainable business practices. For a large, multinational company and its executives, such a task is heroic.

Ray Anderson, who for good reason may be the single most profiled socially responsible businessperson in America, has taken on that task with his billion dollar transnational company Interface, the world's largest manufacturer of commercial carpeting. Anderson is determined to make his company the first industrial company in the whole world to attain environmental sustainability, and then to go beyond simply sustaining, and become restorative to nature.

In his book *Mid-Course Correction*, Anderson writes: "My company's technologies and those of every other company I know of anywhere, in their present forms, are plundering the earth. This cannot go on and on." And this:

> *[B]asic needs must be met in the most resource-efficient ways possible, and meeting basic needs for all must take precedence over providing luxuries for a few. The growing field of spirituality (a term that, frankly, turned me off when I first heard it, because I associated it with religiosity) in business is a cornerstone of the next industrial revolution, as I see it. I believe, too, that the ascendancy of women in business is coming just in the nick of time. It is that instinctive nurturing nature, found more frequently in women, but also present in men if they will allow it to surface, that will recognize and elevate in business the vital, indispensable role of genuine caring. Caring for human capital and natural capital (Earth) as much as we traditionally have cared for financial capital will give social equity and environmental stewardship their rightful places alongside economic progress, and move society to reinvent the means for achieving economic progress itself.*

Interface defines environmental sustainability as "taking nothing from the earth that is not renewable and doing no harm to the biosphere." The company has put its mission on the line by making its progress available for anyone to see online at www.interfaceinc.com.

Stewardship

Peter Block is a well-known business consultant who wrote the most radical theoretical business book I've ever read. *Stewardship*, written in 1993, takes us to the radical core of democracy and the Golden Rule applied to business.

> *Stewardship is defined as the willingness to be accountable for the well-being of the larger organization by operating in service, rather than in control, of those around us....[T]here can be reconciliation of what is good for the soul, good for a customer, and good for the health of the larger institution.*
>
> *Our survival depends on our taking the idea of service to constituents and making it concrete in our governance systems.... Service-based governance strategies mean the redistribution of power, privilege, purpose, and wealth.*
>
> *Patriarchy expresses the belief that it is those at the top who are responsible for the success of the organization and the well-being of its members. A measure of patriarchy is how frequently we use images of parenting to describe how bosses should manage subordinates in organizations. If our intent is to create workplaces that provide meaning, and are economically sound and strong in the marketplace, we need to face the implications for having chosen patriarchy for the governance system inside our organizations. The governance system we have inherited and continue to create is based on sovereignty and a form of intimate colonialism. These are strong terms, but they are essentially accurate. We govern our organizations by valuing above all else, consistency, control, and predictability. These become the means of dominance by which colonialism and sovereignty are enacted.*

Block goes on to describe democracy as being much more than voting every four years. Our current electoral system does not really give us the experience of democracy; although our nation is based politically on democratic values, this has not translated into a democratically based economy, which essentially means we have no real democracy in this country. Whereas democracy is control by the many, in most workplaces power and control are held by the privileged few. Instead of our hope residing in democratically elected leadership, we have turned it over to those with either parental or autocratic power, withering our spirit. Block writes that "we have all created this ruling class by separating those who manage the work from those who do the work."

Havens of Democracy

People these days don't often use the term "patriarchy," but it ultimately refers to asserting dominance, whether by male or female, which is antithetical to true democracy. The only purely democratic workplace I have helped to create and worked in was the Briarpatch Co-op described in chapter 4. With the membership requirement of working eight hours every quarter in the store, the board members, elected by co-op members, were intimately involved with the managers in its operation, and the co-op members themselves, either as shoppers or workers, were in the store constantly, interacting with managers and board members. It was grassroots democracy in its truest sense.

Consumer cooperatives have evolved over the past thirty years with much less active involvement by members, so that many of them are now dominated by a single manager running a traditional, top-down hierarchy with little of the democratic innovation found in even some more progressive small businesses. So the structure of a business does not necessarily define how a company works internally. And no matter the legal structure, as crucial as it may be to whoever wields ultimate control, there are always opportunities to replace dominating structures with pockets of democratic participation. These little pockets, living in the cracks like the Briarpatch, could very well represent the practice we need to ultimately create a fully democratic economy.

In the same way that the daily news emphasizes the negative, the sensational, and the weird, the Darwinian idea of survival of the fittest is often trumpeted as what makes business work. It isn't. It is the positive, the cooperation by people of good will and good cheer, people who live by the Golden Rule, working together, that makes business function. The struggle to understand, to make a contribution, to find meaning is what creates pockets of democratic cooperation in the workplace. The boss may be a tyrant, the workload demands may be unbearable, the fear of not getting the next paycheck may weigh heavily, but the spirit refuses to be subdued. Civility, creativity, responsibility, a helping hand continue to reach out and bridge the chasm of despair that sometimes threatens to overwhelm those who are here to get the work done, to make the deadline, to serve others. The trickle down (it is always just a trickle) of financial rewards can be met by a filtering up of values that matter, that cry for recognition, that demand attention. It will be ignored, derided, challenged, suppressed. It is what democracy is made of, and it will eventually overcome.

It just may be the practice of this informal, unquenchable, innate human cooperation and democratic participation that will ultimately overcome the overarching structures and individuals who exploit it unfairly for financial gain and insist that red-fanged competition is how life works best. Competition is certainly healthy and necessary, but it is only healthy when it is balanced with cooperation.

Although I have yet to repeat the ideal workplace that we experienced once upon a time in the Briarpatch, I think, if asked, that most of the people I have worked with over the years since would say that I did help create little havens of Briarpatch values and ways of working together that were open, inclusive, cooperative, service oriented, hardworking, supportive, effective, meaningful, and fun to be in. And no one woke up the next morning dreading the workday. Sometimes a simple haven is all one needs.

Prudence

"I hold that democracy cannot be evolved by forcible methods," Gandhi wrote.

The spirit of democracy cannot be imposed from without. It has to come from within.... I value individual freedom but you must not forget that man is essentially a social being. He has risen to his present status by learning to adjust his individualism to the requirements of social progress. Unrestricted individualism is the law of the beast of the jungle. We have learnt to strike the mean between individual freedom and social restraint. Willing submission to social restraint for the sake of the well-being of the whole society enriches both the individual and the society of which one is a member. The golden rule of conduct, therefore, is mutual toleration, seeing that we will never all think alike and we shall see truth in fragment and from different angles of vision. Conscience is not the same thing for all. Whilst, therefore, it is a good guide for individual conduct, imposition of that conduct upon all will be an insufferable inter-ference with everybody's freedom of conscience.... I do not believe in the doctrine of the greatest good of the greatest number. It means in its nakedness that in order to achieve the supposed good of 51 percent the interest of 49 percent may be, or rather, should be sacrificed. It is a heart-less doctrine and has done harm to humanity. The only real, dignified, human doctrine is the greatest good of all, and this can only be achieved by uttermost self-sacrifice.

The democratic revolution that resulted in our Constitution and Bill of Rights lies incomplete and unfulfilled. Like our ancestors, the peasants who fled the abuses of royalty and religious orthodoxy, the unsophisticated who rose from the dregs to build a solid middle class of dignity and free choice, we will continually have to defend against the forces of greed and injustice that pretend to be on our side, but have no agenda other than to force us back to their preferred feudalism. An empowered middle class, those who do the work and build the capital, demands too much of the pie according to those who have way more than their share already, and they will forever use their part of the pie to keep grabbing more of it, no matter what the consequences are to our common ground and common wealth.

Meanwhile, we'll be working harder and longer and wonder why we are still getting behind rather than getting ahead. Our jobs will be taken from us and given to others elsewhere without asking our opinion or taking a vote. Our food, air, and water, and, in turn, our bodies will be violated with wastes and poisons despite our protests. Our sons and daughters will be sent to war to kill and die for lies and to help the wealthy garner even more, ever more, never enough.

This is what will continue to happen, that is, unless and until we command a full, living economic democracy. Then our jobs and our economics can be controlled democratically, fulfilling the ultimate dream of full democracy, and our jobs will become more meaningful in the process. It will start with the organization and control of our work and workplaces, as we insist that our personal values, rather than the greed and immorality of the few, become the foundation of leadership and guidance. When democratic control of our jobs and economy becomes real and meaningful, then our politics and our work will become real and meaningful. A creative democracy can bring large corporations back under democratic balance by rescinding their rights as "people," outlawing their corrupting donations to politicians, enforcing the laws against monopolies, and balancing their management structures with blue- and white-collar inclusion, and where appropriate, democratic unionization — including seats on boards of directors.

As citizens, we can pay attention to what we buy, who made it, where it was made, how it was made. We can educate ourselves about which companies care about more than just making profits. We can learn about the companies that genuinely practice good values, that positively influence their local communities, and that don't exploit their workers. We can care more about our relationship with their values, and less about price. That intention in itself makes the world a better place.

This chapter began with the statement that prudence is wisdom and sensibleness in practical matters like business. It counsels caution, moderation, and sound judgment. Creating and joining cooperative alternatives that compete with corporate services will help democratize our business culture. John Dewey writes in his essay "Creative Democracy":

> *[D]emocracy as a way of life is controlled by personal faith in personal day-by-day working together with others. Democracy is the belief that even when needs and ends or consequences are different for each individual, the habit of amicable cooperation — which may include, as in sport, rivalry and competition — is itself a priceless addition to life. To take as far as possible every conflict which arises — and they are bound to arise — out of the atmosphere and medium of force, of violence as a means of settlement into that of discussion and of intelligence is to treat those who disagree — even profoundly — with us as those from whom we may learn, and in so far, as friends.... To cooperate by giving differences a chance to show themselves because of the belief that the expression of difference is not only a right of the other persons but is a means of enriching one's own life-experience, is inherent in the democratic personal way of life.... It is to realize that democracy is a reality only as it is indeed a commonplace of living.... Every other form of moral and social faith rests upon the idea that experience must be subjected at some point or other to some form of external control; to some "authority" alleged to exist outside the processes of experience.*

A more creative democracy would balance the profit motive with the service motive, and balance the top-down corporate structure with the bottom-up cooperative structures. With the power of labor now diminished considerably, the gap between rich and poor continues to widen alarmingly and the middle class is losing its place on the economic ladder. A creative democracy can prevent that from occurring. There are things we can do to reform and enliven what we have now.

The antidote to self-interest is to commit and find a cause, to commit to something outside of ourselves, which is really a passionate commitment to the greater community, to each other. The hunger for commitment lies within each of us.

Meaningful work comes alive
with the prudence of a creative democracy.
And that requires courage....

courage

[creative action heroes]

The real work of planet-saving will be small, humble, and humbling, and (insofar as it involves love) pleasing and rewarding. Its jobs will be too many to count, too many to report, too many to be publicly noticed or rewarded, too small to make anyone rich or famous.

— Wendell Berry

A life of small-scale farming may appear to be primitive, but in living such a life, it becomes possible to contemplate the Great Way. I believe that if one fathoms deeply one's own neighborhood and the everyday world in which he lives, the greatest of all worlds will be revealed.

— Masanobu Fukuoka

Heroism is a courageous response of the heart that can show a person's true character. It can be the response in a brief moment, as when a firefighter enters a burning building to rescue a child, or when some ordinary person walking along a beach suddenly dives into the water to rescue a drowning stranger. The character and ideals of a hero may not be apparent in an individual for many years of ordinary life. Then, suddenly, a challenge is presented that calls for an instant decision that could mean risking one's own life to save another's, and in that moment when the challenge is accepted the heart of a true hero is unveiled. Or the heroic heart may be revealed through a lifetime devoted to a great cause, such as standing up and fighting for the rights of the downtrodden.

My Creative Action Heroes live their ideals through creating alternatives that solve social problems and make a positive difference in the world. They understand that we cannot know the real world by merely studying it or analyzing it, that instead we must feel it and act in it. Obviously, courageous Creative Action Heroes include Martin Luther King Jr. and Cesar Chavez, highly visible leaders who spearheaded movements involving thousands of other less heralded Creative Action Heroes. They met the daily challenges of building and maintaining positive social change.

But there are also less well-known Creative Action Heroes, like former University of California, Santa Cruz, professor Paul Lee, who not only brought Alan Chadwick to his university (see chapter 2) but also helped create the Homeless Garden Project in Santa Cruz, which goes well beyond charity to solve a social problem. The project employs and trains homeless people within a community-supported organic garden enterprise. This meaningful work environment helps to build self-esteem, responsibility, and self-sufficiency. It integrates homeless people and the community within the security and beauty of a productive garden. The project works to help people solve their *own* problems. In the words of one graduate, "We don't need someone to carry us — we need someone who's willing to get us on our feet."

Creative Action Heroes may also be independent writers like Wendell Berry and Gene Logsdon, who went back to their roots on farms to apply their lives to "experiments in living" and publish their carefully gained insights for us to admire and possibly emulate. They spawned thousands of other Creative Action Heroes who read their books and courageously left safe, steady jobs to raise healthy food on small farms when other small farmers were being forced off their land by industrial agriculture.

All these people, both well-known and unknown, sung and unsung, are heroic because, among other admirable character traits, they *live* an enduring set of values. This web of heroes, great and small, who move humankind ever forward by the work they do and the lives they lead, reminds us that no matter how bleak life may seem, how anxious or depressed we may become, someone somewhere is making a choice to give and make a positive difference anyway. Getting involved is in itself transforming. I'm inspired by those who care enough to create real alternatives by putting their lives on the line for a better way of working and living, and never, ever giving up.

Follow the Food

For me, farming, agriculture, and food are more than the fundamental underpinning of human life. Understanding what has happened, and is still happening, to our agriculture gives us insights into our ailing civilization and its cure. If we want to find the culprits who are destroying the environment and nature, we follow the money. When we do that, we find that a lot of money leads to the agriculture and chemical industries. So we follow the food.

In the book *Fatal Harvest*, Andrew Kimbrell identifies seven central myths of industrial agriculture. ("Myths" here mean untruth, rather than Joseph Campbell's deeper definition of myth as a symbol of truth.) The evidence, carefully researched and documented, is overwhelming and irrefutable:

MYTH ONE — *Industrial Agriculture Will Feed the World*

THE TRUTH — *World hunger is not created by lack of food but by poverty and landlessness, which deny people access to food. Industrial agriculture actually increases hunger by raising the cost of farming, by forcing tens of millions of farmers off the land, and by growing primarily high-profit export and luxury crops.*

MYTH TWO — *Industrial Food Is Safe, Healthy, and Nutritious*

THE TRUTH — *Industrial agriculture contaminates our vegetables and fruits with pesticides, slips dangerous bacteria into our lettuce, and puts genetically engineered growth hormones into our milk. It is not surprising that cancer, food-borne illnesses, and obesity are at an all-time high.*

MYTH THREE — *Industrial Food Is Cheap*

THE TRUTH — *If you added the real cost of industrial food — its health, environmental, and social costs — to the current supermarket price, not even our wealthiest citizens could afford to buy it.*

MYTH FOUR — *Industrial Agriculture Is Efficient*

THE TRUTH — *Small farms produce more agricultural output per unit area than large farms. Moreover, larger, less diverse farms require far more mechanical and chemical inputs. These ever increasing inputs are devastating to the environment and make these farms far less efficient than smaller, more sustainable farms.*

MYTH FIVE — *Industrial Food Offers More Choices*

THE TRUTH — *What the consumer actually gets in the supermarket is an illusion of choice. Food labeling does not even tell us what pesticides are on our food or what products have been genetically engineered. Most importantly, the myth of choice masks the tragic loss of tens of thousands of crop varieties caused by industrial agriculture.*

MYTH SIX — *Industrial Agriculture Benefits the Environment and Wildlife*

THE TRUTH — *Industrial agriculture is the largest single threat to the earth's biodiversity. Fence-row-to-fence-row plowing, planting, and harvesting techniques decimate wildlife habitats, while massive chemical use poisons the soil and water, and kills off countless plant and animal communities.*

MYTH SEVEN — *Biotechnology Will Solve the Problems of Industrial Agriculture*

THE TRUTH — *New biotech crops will not solve industrial agriculture's problems, but will compound them and consolidate control of the world's food supply in the hands of a few large corporations. Biotechnology will destroy biodiversity and food security, and drive self-sufficient farmers off their land.*

It's clear that if we follow the food, we find that industrial agriculture is at the root of much that ails our planet. But as corporate agriculture MegaMaws have plundered and poisoned our bodies and our planet, there are those who said, "No, that's not the way to go. That's not the way *I'm* going to go."

Heroes' Path

George Bernard Shaw said: "This is the true joy of life, the being used for a purpose recognized by yourself as a mighty one; the being thoroughly worn out before you are thrown on the scrap heap; the being a force of Nature instead of a feverish, selfish little clod of ailments and grievances complaining that the world will not devote itself to making you happy.... The only real tragedy in life is being used by personally minded men for purposes that you recognize to be ignoble."

To illustrate the work of Creative Action Heroes, I want to focus now on people who are confronting head-on this devastation to our agricultural health. This immense challenge has required Creative Action Heroes to find and match their purpose with what is needed by the community. Wherever someone has the courage to step out against the conventional wisdom when it is wrong and start doing things differently, there you'll find a Creative Action Hero. Wherever courageous action to better life on Earth attracts the scorn, the laughter, the shaking of heads among "those who know how it's supposed to be done," there you'll find a Creative Action Hero. Wherever creative action follows the values of the wisdom traditions, of the Golden Rule, of gentleness and patience, of playing fair, of humility, compassion, and peace, there you'll find a Creative Action Hero.

When Rachel Carson's exposé *Silent Spring* was published in 1962, many people were alarmed at what great environmental harm was being done by chemical pesticides in nature and in our food. Many had no idea what should be done, but a few decided to start doing something about it. Some began raising the issue with their government representatives, others began organizing to fight the chemical companies' massive pollution with publicity and protests. And a tiny few decided not to wait for the government to take care of the problem but to start doing things differently by growing, selling, and serving food without the poison. These were the pioneers of the organic food movement.

The Creative Action Heroes portrayed here are people I know personally. But they stand in for many, many others who have the courage and wisdom to solve serious social problems through their daily work. You may feel that it is too provincial to focus on one market segment in one part of the country. There are so many different Creative Action Heroes in many different fields. You would be right, of course, and covering even a fraction of the work they do would require a book in itself. But supporting local businesses and local farms is of growing importance, and by narrowing our focus to an important effort concentrated in a community, we can explore, in depth, who these heroes are and celebrate their importance to their community.

For me, organic family farmers model the answer to many of our social problems by learning from and cooperating with nature rather than working against it; by practicing nurturance rather than dominance; by valuing long-term sustainability rather than short-term exploitation.

Apply their values to our growing energy problems and we'll solve global warming, soaring energy costs, and resource wars by developing renewable, sustainable energy resources. Organic farming itself actually reduces global warming by encouraging beneficial organic matter, which takes carbon dioxide, the primary greenhouse gas, from the atmosphere and fixes it in the soil. According to extensive research over many years at the Rodale Institute:

> *If only 10,000 medium sized farms in the U.S. converted to organic production, they would store so much carbon in the soil that it would be equivalent to taking 1,174,400 cars off the road, or reducing car miles driven by 14.62 billion. Converting the U.S.'s 160 million corn and soybean acres to organic production would sequester enough carbon to satisfy 73 percent of the Kyoto targets for CO2 reduction in the U.S. U.S. agriculture as currently practiced emits a total of 1.5 trillion pounds of CO2 annually into the atmosphere. Converting all U.S. cropland to organic would not only wipe out agriculture's massive emission problem. By eliminating energy-costly chemical fertilizers, it would actually give us a net increase in soil carbon of 734 billion pounds.*

Apply organic farmers' values to our culture and we resolve racial, ethnic, and religious prejudice by embracing diversity and difference, rather than bigoted, divisive adherence to rigid belief systems resulting in conflict and wars. OrganicConsumers.org: "According to the largest review yet done of studies comparing organic to conventional agriculture, organic farming [in Great Britain] increases biodiversity at every level, from bacteria to birds to mammals. The two groups that conducted the reviews — English Nature, a government group, and the Royal Society for the Protection of Birds — had no vested interest in organic farming. They concluded that organic farming fosters biodiversity by using fewer inorganic fertilizers and pesticides and by adopting critter-friendly practices like mixing arable and livestock farming."

Apply organic farmers' values to health and we learn that nurturing the soil that nature has provided results in strong plants with built-in disease prevention and pest protection that, in turn, build strength, prevention, and protection into our bodies rather than assaulting them with chemical poisons that wreak havoc and encourage disease.

Nurturance and cooperation, the values of care and love, rather than dominance and competition, the values of fear and war. I find these people and their lives awe-inspiring. As I've mentioned, I didn't grow up on a farm and I've never lived on one. But my grandparents were farmers and my admiration for the work and importance of small farmers is in my genes.

A Healthy Respect

One of my dearest friends, Charles Martin, is an organic farmer, a lean, spry youngster of seventy-four years with a twinkle in his eye and some thoughts about farming, food, and health that are definitely not mainstream. For many years he and his wife, Catherine, ran a small biodynamic/organic farm in Comptche, California, near the Mendocino coast, supplying their neighbors and local restaurants. They also operated a nonprofit health foundation. They now live in very active retirement near Willits, California.

As a boy growing up in Whittier, in Southern California, Charles was interested in gardening and farming, and in high school he had a job milking cows on a dairy farm. Inducted into the Korean War, he was seriously injured. The drugs and antibiotics administered to him for his injury further damaged his health. After graduating from mechanical engineering school and going to work for Boeing in Seattle, he began exploring his health problems and was advised by a homeopathic specialist in degenerative diseases that he needed to "get back to nature, get off all refined foods, grow your own organic produce, get your water from clean springs, buy a juicer, grind your own flour, and eat naturally." The doctor told him that his body could gradually repair itself over time if it was fed properly. That advice changed his life.

I stopped by to see Charles a while back, and as we chatted about his farm and about health in general, I asked him what he had learned from changing his diet so many years ago.

I'm convinced that health comes from the soil, from what we eat and the quality of what we eat. I had kidney problems, backaches, ulcers, you name it. By my late twenties, eating mostly from our backyard organic garden, I was back in very good shape.

I've always gardened and farmed for health reasons, not for commercial reasons. There are certain compromises I won't make because of that. Biodynamics is a sustainable way of organic farming with nature. If you start taking shortcuts you start having health problems on the farm. When I first started farming I had a few plant disease problems, a few insect problems like cabbage worms and coddling moth, but as the years went on, things kept getting better until we had no disease problems or insect problems. Cabbage worms were controlled by an old green tree frog that I had out in the garden and by hornets that lived in the area, and the ground toads took care of the earwigs and mealy bugs, so I had a nice balance of nature built up. I had shelter belts and habitats and water dishes in the garden for the frogs so they didn't have to leave to cool off. The tree frog would sit in the cabbage patch devouring cabbage worms, a big worm in his mouth and a grin on his face. It was a real joy to be a part of that.

I wasn't interested in selling our produce to people who didn't appreciate the effort that I put into it. I'd go to farmers' markets, but many there are just looking for the lowest price — I didn't have time for that. I spent too much time raising good quality, tasty produce. I just would not quibble over price. There were too many customers who appreciated what I was doing. I feel that if you're looking to save money on food, then you're going to pay for it in doctor bills later on. That's not the way we wanted to live.

Both our farming and our health counseling were based on the idea of soil and health because if you grow healthy soils you'll have healthy plants, and if you have healthy plants you'll have healthy animals, and therefore healthy people who eat those plants and animals. It's really that simple. Health is natural in nature, and this nonsense that disease is a normal way of life is just not true. It's because you're not living according to nature's laws that you get sick. If you just go back to nature's laws, you'll find that these problems will be controlled naturally and you won't have to depend on drugs and high technology.

We counsel the use of a healing diet of vegetarian, organic raw foods, and juices. If you are really ill, we believe you should just fast — stop eating for a while and let the body do its own healing by ridding itself of toxins. And it really does work, whether you have arthritis, tuberculosis, colds, tonsillitis. Disease is the body's attempt to rid itself of poisons because of our eating habits. I don't have any strong views against eating good healthy meat, but I've come to be vegetarian myself for health reasons.

I do not believe that germs cause disease. Germs are nature's scavengers coming in to clean up sick waste materials that you have in your body. The same principle applies in the garden. Plant disease and insects are attempting to clean up an unhealthy situation in the garden. Nature is consistent. The drug company's answer is to kill the messenger, the germ, just as the pesticide company's answer is to kill the insect. In both cases the hosts, whether it is the plant or the body, is the problem. The plant needs to be strengthened by good soil practices, the body needs to be strengthened by good nutrition. Then they each will be strong enough to deal with the problem.

We had a couple of apprentices at our farm who came here with health problems. Both boys had severe environmental illnesses and had been to the best medical clinics. Nothing helped. They had been given drugs, cortisones, antihistamines. They were in devitalized states, one a walking skeleton, the other hyperallergic to everything. They went through an educational program at the farm, learned to eat raw foods. One went on a twenty-eight day fast on water, the other went on two fasts of ten days and seventeen days. Before the hyperallergic boy left after six *months, he had worked sixty hours in the hot fields of Albion harvesting hay and never sneezed once. He couldn't believe it. The other one is doing well, last we heard, and knows exactly what to do if symptoms come back after eating junk food. It was amazing to see.*

My spirituality is very important to me. I reverence and respect God's creation. Catherine and I look upon our roles here in life as stewards. We feel that we have a responsibility to our Creator to care for the Creation, to nurture it, and look after it. And this includes our bodies. . . . Spirituality plays a central part of our whole philosophy of farming as well. I believe in treating animals well, providing them with a natural environment and a natural diet. They should be allowed to range free and be treated with gentleness and kindness. I don't think we could ever do it any differently. We feel that this is the way our Creator wants us to live. He's created this wonderful world for us, and living in harmony with nature's spiritual and moral laws is where peace really comes from.

Dominate or Cultivate?

The most fundamental of businesses, and one whose values I believe come closest to those taught by traditional wisdom, is organic family farming. As I wrote earlier, I've found my own Creative Action Heroes among the peasants and those who look at life with the peasant's perspective — organic market farmers, organic restaurateurs, and others involved with the organic food movement. Their mission, and the missions of their businesses, address a problem, either directly or indirectly, that touches all of our lives: environmental pollution from toxic chemicals on the land, in our water, and in our food that cause health problems.

Our culture's idyllic idea of the small farm features the white farmhouse with the red barn, chickens clucking in the barnyard, pastured animals munching sleepily on green hills, and the farmer rocking gently on the front porch at dusk. Of course, nothing could be further from the truth. A small organic or sustainable farm is a beehive of swarming activity from before first light until way after the sun has disappeared. I remember reading somewhere that 70 percent of Americans, if they had the choice, would live on a farm. Whether or not they would choose to work that farm is another matter entirely.

The accumulated and applied knowledge, technical expertise, and wisdom needed to be a successful organic farmer would rank at the very top of any professional intelligence scale. Nature, weather, business, sales, animal husbandry, veterinary medicine, plant science, insect behavior, pest management, soil chemistry, mechanics, electrical repair, carpentry, forest management, building codes, transport, markets, food storage, refrigeration — all are skill and knowledge areas that a good farmer masters. Throw in the physical demands and the traditional values of hard work and community involvement, and we've got the unsung cultural heroes who grow and harvest our food organically.

And they aren't just men. Women now run almost 15 percent of American farms, up from 5 percent in 1978, and that trend is even more pronounced with organic farms, where 22 percent are managed by women. Organic farmers work symbiotically with nature — cultivating a relationship of mutual benefit and dependence — as a vocation, and as craft and service, the way it's been done for thousands and thousands of years. Their craft is nurturance.

In stark contrast, businesspersons whose values, I feel, are some of the furthest removed from those of traditional wisdom work in corporate industrial agribusiness. They work against nature, exploiting nature, dictating to nature, removed from nature in their palaces of steel and glass. They poison our land, run thousands of acres of monocrops, rain down their destruction and poisons on peasant farmers in other countries, taking away their livelihoods of subsistence farming and casting them destitute without hope. Every problem, from insect infestation to weed control, is dealt with by chemicals and poisons indiscriminately spread over land and water, and served on our plates at home with no notice or regret.

Agrarian Ideals and Values

Although our food is now produced by less than 2 percent of the population, we are almost completely dependent on services that we take for granted but ignore at our peril. What is the perspective that generates and is generated by such craft? Wendell Berry's description of the agrarian mind goes a long way toward illuminating the values of the small organic farmer. "The agrarian mind begins with the love of fields and ramifies in good farming, good cooking, good eating, and gratitude to God," writes Wendell Berry about agrarian values versus the approach of industrial farming. The agrarian mind conserves and treasures the miracle of life and circulates whatever moderate economic gains are produced primarily within the local community and region that create them. That system of values contrasts unfavorably with the "industrial-economic" mind, which evolves giant global enterprises that value only the exploitation of resources for economic gain.

The agrarian ideal, Berry continues, does not "propose that everybody should be a farmer or that we do not need cities" or manufacturing enterprises. It only insists that enterprise is "scaled to fit the local landscape, the local ecosystem, and the local community, and that it should be locally owned and employ local people." It would insist that ownership share in the "fate of the place and its community" by having to "live with the results of their decisions." Most certainly, these constructive and purposeful goals point us in the direction of meaningful choices in our lives. Agrarian ideals value quality, while the industrial ideal values quantity and primarily profit. There have been many benefits from industrialism's single-minded focus on efficient production, but quality has not been one of them.

Cultivate

Compared to chemical agriculture, organic agriculture is more efficient and produces less expensively (when all costs are considered) healthier, more nutritious food. It can feed the world far better and far more cheaply. Industrial agriculture is unsafe and is destroying our health, our environment, and our wildlife.

Organic food is more expensive because industrial agriculture is subsidized by our tax dollars, its costs are externalized into our environment, and chemical poison applications are less expensive than hand labor. Organic farmers are on their own. According to the book *Fatal Harvest*: "Small farms almost always produce far more agricultural output per unit area than larger farms. According to a 1992 U.S. Agricultural Census report, relatively smaller farm sizes are two to ten times more productive per unit acre than larger ones. The smallest farms surveyed in the study, those of twenty-seven acres or less, are more than ten times as productive (in dollar output per acre) than large farms (six thousand acres or more), and extremely small farms (four acres or less) can be over a hundred times as productive."

Then there is the safety issue. When we send farmworkers into fields to mix and apply chemical poisons without training them or protecting them from harm we must ask ourselves, is that how we would like to be treated? When a farmer knowingly, and unnecessarily, applies poisons to strawberries, for example, that will be served by unsuspecting mothers to their beloved children, we must ask ourselves, is that how a self-respecting pillar of the community carries out his responsibilities to his neighbors?

Our government has found thirty-six pesticides on 90 percent of the strawberries it tested: 2,4-D; acephate; anilazine; azinphosmethyl; benomyl; BHC; bifenthrin; captan; carbaryl; chlordanes; chlorothalonil; DCPA; DDT; diazinon; dichlorvos (DDVP); dicofol; dieldrin; dimethoate; diphenylamine (DPA); endosulfan; fenpropathrin; fenvalerate; folpet; heptachlor; iprodione; malathion; metalaxyl; methamidophos; methidathion; methomyl; myclobutanil; oxamyl; piperonyl butoxide; propargite; thiabendazole; and triadimefon.

These pesticides are proven carcinogens, damage reproductive systems, interfere with hormones, and damage the brain and the nervous and immune systems. Some are systemic and cannot be washed off. Some of these poisons are now being bioengineered to grow as part of the plant itself. And they are all totally unnecessary and should be eliminated immediately from our foods.

Felipe

Organic food is not a luxury. In addition to the dangers I've listed above, agricultural pesticides have been linked to terrible birth defects. Organic farming can make the difference between life and death for those working in the fields.

Felipe Franco was born with no limbs in the San Joaquin Valley. His farmworker mother sued a chemical company and won a settlement. She had worked in the fields since the beginning of pregnancy near Bakersfield, and among the pesticides used was one structurally similar to thalidomide, a drug that had caused thousands of horrible birth defects in Europe. No one had told her what they were using or how it could affect her.

So who is responsible for Felipe's disfigurement? The consumer was just trying to get the best price, as was the produce buyer. The farmer was just trying to make a living. The chemical salesman was just doing his job. The chemist was just fascinated by how effectively a poison could kill a pest. Who will take responsibility?

Before poisons arrive on our plates and begin taking their toll on our health, those who grow and harvest it take the first risks. Migrant children work beside pregnant mothers on land saturated with methyl bromide, a potent nerve toxin that causes birth defects and brain damage in animals. When I worked for the UFW in Delano, there were continuous reports of stillbirths and miscarriages among migrant workers, which were not reported because workers were afraid of losing their jobs.

That's why I feel that organic farming is a life-and-death matter, a matter of values, and a moral choice, and that's why working with organics became my vocational mission and my personal discovery of meaningful work. And I have a confession to make. I am almost as fanatic about organic as my true-believer dad was about his religion. He not only had neon signs flashing his belief system, he also advertised on our family car. He cut out letters from red reflective tape and stuck them on the back bumper, spelling out: "God Saves and Heals." When he drove me to my junior high because I missed the bus, I would ask him to please drop me off around the corner, fearing that one of my buddies would make fun of me. And now look! My car sports a sticker on the bumper reading "Bring Organic Home" and another in the back window, "Support Organic Agriculture" — my own version of how to save the world. Better keep me away from neon so I don't embarrass anybody.

Common Sense

At the heart of everything that the organic movement holds true is the belief that we should first do no harm. Many of my Creative Action Heroes are people whose values and lifework are predicated on an awareness of how current farming methods do harm and taking responsibility for changing them. For example, research has shown that there may be several contributing factors to the explosion of cancers, brain tumors, and other debilitating diseases that are wrecking the lives of our friends and families. One of them, carcinogenic environmental pollutants, was documented first by Rachel Carson, whose research was followed up recently by Sandra Steingraber in her book *Living Downstream*.

"According to the most recent tally, forty possible carcinogens appear in drinking water, sixty are released by industry into ambient air, and sixty-six are routinely sprayed on food crops as pesticides," Steingraber writes. "[T]he elimination of a great number of them would reduce the carcinogenic burden we all bear and thus would prevent considerable suffering and loss of human life."

Most people still do not connect environmental problems with their own declining health, but millions suffer from the onslaught of health problems caused by the stuff we swallow. Our foods are sprayed, irradiated, refined, and stripped of nutrients; our soil is deficient in minerals because of modern farming methods; and artificial additives and chemicals are inserted at every step of production to increase shelf life and add flavors that are missing because of our processing.

Besides the land used for growing and providing food, the beautiful expanses of green turf maintained for recreation are also often saturated by chemical poisons. The typical golf course uses four times the amount of pesticides per acre than an agricultural field, and golf course superintendents, like farmers, have excess rates of lymphoma as well as cancers of the brain and prostate. Pesticides used on golf course lawns are completely unnecessary, as proved by the growing number of golf courses in New York and elsewhere that have gone completely chemical-free.

We may not have much personal control over the pollutants around us in the environment, but we do have control over what we put in and on our bodies, and common sense would dictate that we keep our personal intake of pollutants to a minimum.

Bringing It Home

Pesticide use may seem like something distant from our homes, centered in the far-off fields of large farms. But how many of us use pesticides on our lawns and gardens? Dr. Marion Moses, who ran the Farmworker Clinic in Delano when I was there, went on to found the Pesticide Education Center in San Francisco. Her research on lawn care pesticides shows the following:

Many lawn care pesticides are known or suspected to cause cancer, birth defects, and infertility. They can also damage the brain and nervous system, lungs, kidneys, liver, and endocrine and immune systems. Pesticides used on your lawn or your neighbor's can end up inside your home even when the windows are closed. Pesticide residues are tracked indoors by family members and pets, and they drift in through cracks and crevices and small openings around windows and doorways. Once inside they can stay there for a long time, contaminating furniture, upholstery, carpets, even children's toys. Pesticide residues last much longer indoors, for months or even years — since there is no direct sunlight, air, wind, or rain to break them down or wash them away. The highest levels are found in house dust, especially carpet dust.

Lawn care pesticides are easily absorbed into the body, especially through the skin. Children crawling or playing on lawns and carpets or with toys that have been contaminated readily absorb pesticides through the skin and by swallowing. Children absorb 100 percent more pesticides when their hands and skin are wet than when their hands and skin are dry. Children are much more susceptible to the health effects of pesticides than adults. At the same level of exposure they will absorb more pesticides because they have more skin surface for their size and take in more breaths per minute.

Just because you do not get any recognizable symptoms from pesticides does not mean you are not being exposed and are not at risk. Long-term effects such as cancer and brain damage, especially in children, may occur from low-level exposures over time.

Lawn care pesticides can cause short-term (acute) effects, including rashes, burning of the eyes and throat, breathing problems, and flulike symptoms such as headache, nausea, muscle aches, and fatigue. They can also aggravate or cause asthma, allergies, and multiple chemical sensitivity. Long term (chronic) effects linked to pesticides include cancer, infertility, birth defects, Parkinson's disease, and damage to the brain and nervous system. The types of pesticide-caused cancer seen in children include leukemia, brain cancer, non-Hodgkin's lymphoma, and soft tissue sarcoma. The same cancers are seen in adults, as are multiple myeloma and cancer of the pancreas, breast, prostate, kidney/bladder, eye, and colon-rectum.

Fortunately, Dr. Moses has tips for a healthy, nontoxic lawn: "Remember that before the aggressive marketing of toxic lawn chemicals, Americans did have beautiful natural lawns. They did it by using common sense and working with natural ecosystems, not destroying them. . . . Many people are under the false impression that glyphosate (Roundup) and other herbicides are not pesticides. Do not give your lawn 'junk food' by using chemical fertilizers, which greens it up but stresses the lawn and makes it more vulnerable to pests. Use compost and natural organic materials instead."

Even if you are not concerned for yourself, your use of lawn chemicals can put your neighbors at risk. Most pesticides never reach the target pest; 85 to 90 percent drift off target, traveling a mile or more and contaminating the surrounding air, water, soil, other people's property, and children's play areas. Your lawn chemical use can make other people sick and expose to risk pregnant women, cancer survivors, the elderly, and other people who are on medication or have serious health problems.

So what are our choices? Let's look at the Canadian example. As awareness about the problems with lawn care pesticides rose in Canada, individual towns began banning their use. The chemical companies went to the Supreme Court of Canada to stop it. The Supreme Court upheld the ban, stating, "our common future, that of every Canadian community, depends on a healthy environment."

Clearly, change starts with people learning the facts and demanding change. But it won't happen without a fight. It's a painful personal irony to me that the Scotts Company, which now owns the company with my name on it, Smith & Hawken, is the biggest name in the lawn pesticide business. It has joined with other chemical companies such as Dow Chemical, Syngenta, and ChemLawn to fund a nonprofit front group with the misleading name Project EverGreen. They are running full-page ads stating: "The Gloves Are Off. Because of activists, extremists, and misinformed politicians, consumers are questioning whether the products and resources (such as water) used to care for their lawns, landscapes, and other green spaces are a waste — or a harm to the environment. Yes, legislation and regulations have been throwing the green industry some rough punches. And we're fighting back."

Where is the Golden Rule here? How can a person who knows the research and facts, or at least is responsible for knowing the facts, continue to work for and promote poisons doing this kind of damage to their neighbors, and to all of us?

First Do No Harm

I'm going to return to our organic berry farmer, Jim Cochran. It takes the courage and commitment of a valiant hero to go against the conventional wisdom of farming when your income and survival are at stake, and Jim is such a hero. His farm, Swanton Berry Farm, is the industry leader in developing organic methods for growing strawberries. Since the farm's inception in 1983, Jim and his coworkers began experimenting with alternatives to fumigation with methyl bromide and the other chemicals widely used on strawberries. After a period of experimentation that lasted through 1985, they became completely organic in their production methods. They have been certified by California Certified Organic Farmers since 1987, making them the pioneer of certified organic strawberry farming in California. In 2002, Swanton Berry Farm was awarded the EPA's Stratospheric Ozone Protection Award for being the "pioneer...in developing the technology of farming strawberries...without relying on the soil fumigant methyl bromide," a major contributor to the depletion of the ozone layer.

(An aside: U.S. methyl bromide consumption will continue to increase despite provisions in the Montreal Protocol in 1997 to eliminate production and use of the fumigant in industrial nations by 2005. The United States requested and received permission to increase exemptions that will allow it to use more of this cancer-causing and ozone-depleting chemical than was used by all U.S. agricultural and other users in 2003 on the grounds that there were no good substitutes to replace it.)

Swanton Berry Farm's farming methods rest on two foundations: soil building and crop diversity. The farm has a long-term soil-building program that involves adding biodynamic (biologically inoculated) compost and kelp products, and a crop diversity program that involves growing and incorporating cover crops, usually a grain and a legume. Several years are spent building the soil before the strawberries are planted. Swanton also rotates its crops around fields to avoid the buildup of any one soil pathogen. The idea is not to eliminate pathogens completely, but just to try and encourage the "good guys" in the soil's biologic profile. The crop rotation program helps manage the insect populations as well because several different kinds of plants can be growing in any one field. In addition, "good bugs" are attracted by planting flowers.

Although Swanton Berry Farm was alone in the organic strawberry business in the early days, a few berry farmers are now switching to organic production. As in every other crop, there are no longer any excuses for farmers poisoning our farm communities, farmworkers, and eaters.

An article in the *San Jose Mercury News* describes the battle to outlaw methyl bromide:

> *In the past 10 years, more than $100 million has been spent studying alternatives by the USDA, California, and the strawberry industry, said Rodger Wasson, president of the California Strawberry Commission in Watsonville.... The organic market is expanding. Still, only 2 percent of strawberry acres statewide are organic....[Organic grower] Vanessa Bogenholm rotates her crops every three years to reduce disease. She weeds by hand and uses organic fertilizers, such as seaweed extracts, which must be churned into the soil manually rather than sprayed or introduced with drip irrigation. "It is much more difficult to grow organic," she said. "I've had farmers tell me, 'I don't want to work that hard.'"*

And there is the problem right there. Some in agribusiness would rather poison us and the Earth rather than work that hard. They would rather spend $100 million of our taxpayer dollars trying to come up with another poison they can sell, rather than just calling Jim Cochran and asking him how to do without it.

Clearly what these farmers and institutions are doing is irresponsible, harmful, and needless. "We must hold a man amenable to reason for the choice of his daily craft or profession," Emerson wrote. "It is not an excuse any longer for his deeds that they are the custom of his trade. What business has he with an evil trade? Has he not a calling in his character?"

But the difficulty of bucking the system is immense. Growing organic berries is one thing. Finding a market is another. Just as it took a Jim Cochran to courageously pioneer organic strawberry farming, it took equally courageous pioneers to create a market for them.

Service

I first met Jesse Cool in the early seventies when she became a member of the Briarpatch Co-op. She was a flower child from Pennsylvania with a purple streak in her hair that announced her flair and independent spirit. She would come into Briarpatch Co-op in her bangles and beads to work off her membership hours at the cash register. It wasn't too long before she and her husband were running a restaurant next to the railroad tracks in Menlo Park called Late for the Train, and not too long after that, as Silicon Valley exploded with wealth and importance, she was a celebrity entrepreneur with three of her own award-winning restaurants, a cooking column in the local newspaper, appearances on national TV shows, and a series of cookbooks.

Jesse has been a passionate pioneer and tireless promoter dedicated to organic food and local farming from the beginning, long before it was fashionable. Her restaurants save all compostable waste, which goes back into building soil. In her book *Your Organic Kitchen: The Essential Guide to Selecting and Cooking Organic Foods*, she writes:

"My heroes remain the growing legend of organic farmers — environmental pioneers — who with commitment and vision have chosen the old way, opting for compost and other natural fertilizers to create healthy soils that yield healthy plants. Using integrated pest management, they control pests with beneficial insects, not pesticides. They rotate crops to maintain the soil's fertility. They provide certified organic feed to their cows and chickens. . . . I hope someday, organic farmers will grow all the food that we eat."

We became reacquainted years later, kindred souls dedicated to organics, and I would occasionally hang out at her cozy Flea Street Café while she bustled around the kitchen, greeted customers, and held court at the bar as a cluster of friends and diners would drink wine, eat great food, joke around, and sometimes discuss serious issues of the day.

On one of the slow nights we were sitting at the bar, having one of those quiet conversations that good wine seems to encourage, and I asked her why she had chosen to strike out on such an uncommon path and stay so dedicated to it all these years:

My mom encouraged me to be a free spirit. I mean, how many moms would say, "You need a bit more fuchsia in your hair," and "You have great legs, wear short skirts."? She is nurturing and soft and taught me basic good values about life. She was so honest about love and sex and what and who she was. She taught me to love myself, which is harder for me to do than she made it seem.

I suppose my real philosophy is to live each day fully, to try to not have too many nights where the dark is filled with concern, sleeplessness, heartache, but rather to end each day, as difficult or challenging as it might be, knowing that a new day will happen and I have each and every one of those new days to move ahead, create, change, and be fully alive.

Deep down I am basic blue-collar, and both my parents were salt of the earth and genuine. Being Jewish and Italian, food was both demon and blessing; feeding others is a part of my heritage. My dad owned a grocery store and my uncle had the local slaughterhouse. My parents both taught me to connect to my community, to love fully, to eat to abandon, and to make my work meaningful and a part of my life.

Sometimes I feel so useless. I am an intuitive businessperson and just beginning to learn the basics of business, nearly thirty years into it — how embarrassing! I probably live far more in a place where I feel like I don't do enough, am not effective enough, not good enough, smart enough, giving enough. I think I know how to keep changing things, to move and groove and figure out how to stay alive in a rapidly changing world, maintaining my ethics, my connections, my beliefs, but it's a daily challenge. I hate it when I am not as organized, present, focused as I should be. It is unfair to others and I know it. What's kept me going on the path is that I know what my businesses do with food, and that service and connection to community and environment is right livelihood, and I feel blessed.

Through work I get to really see myself and life. I started working at the age of twelve in my dad's store. It was a remarkable place in the poorest neighborhood of the small coal-mining town in Pennsylvania where I was brought up. My father taught me to work hard and to make that my life. In the end, he actually collapsed and died at a Sunday Farmers' Market. He peddled produce, flirted with the women, told dumb jokes, and was so damn honest it made me crazy. He was a good man and he loved and was loved in every community where he lived.

I always worked, my kids had to work hard, and we all understand that to work hard is good. I could never spend my work time doing something that was not a part of my soulfulness. It has to be integrated in my life. I love work; though challenging, it gives me pleasure and meaning. Work and family go hand in hand for me, and I know richness beyond compare in my work and with my family, who have taught me joy, humor, to be real, and to love, love, love.

I'm not afraid to die, especially if it is at a moment where I am in the midst of an adventure. Adventure can be crawling around the rim of a volcano filled with terror, or being close to someone at dinner.

Courage is exhibited when someone strikes out into unfamiliar territory where few if any have yet gone, and helps pioneer a new way of working and serving. Creative Action Heroes blaze new trails despite what everyone else around them is doing, and whether or not others join, they do what they see is right, at whatever sacrifice. When someone lives originally and courageously, it inspires others to examine their own lives and actions and find within themselves the courage to follow their own original paths.

Organics for Health

Organics is not just about avoiding poisons; it's also about eating well. Researchers in Italy found that organic peaches and pears had higher levels of the health-enhancing antioxidants ascorbic acid and polyphenol than fruits grown with poisons, and researchers at the University of California, Davis, bolstered these claims with a subsequent study, which found that organically grown corn had over 50 percent more ascorbic acid than corn grown with conventional methods. Strawberries and marionberries (a type of blackberry) analyzed in the study had two to six times more antioxidants overall. And according to a study at Tufts University, organic produce, free of toxic chemicals, has a nutrient content approximately 88 percent greater than conventional produce.

Researchers speculate that antioxidants are part of the plants' natural defense mechanisms, and organically grown plants have to rely more on their own defenses to fight off pests and diseases, whereas their chemically pampered counterparts do not. Once eaten, these antioxidants continue the good fight inside our bodies, fending off free radicals that cause cell damage, which can lead to cancer. The Italian researchers found that antioxidants also prevented spoilage and extended the shelf life of organically grown foods. Researchers have also found that the skins of fruits and vegetables contain the highest levels of antioxidants, whereas with conventional produce consumers often peel off the skins in order to avoid as much pesticides as possible.

Organic family farmers have loads of common sense. In this

land of confusion and debate and misinformation and propaganda, they simply say: if you work *with* nature instead of *against* her you will be rewarded with health and abundance. It's just common sense.

Buying organic is a way to make social progress with our purchasing power, to give a donation to our environment with every purchase. Sandra Steingraber recently wrote: "Virtually all the groceries Jeff and I buy for our family are organically grown. As well as an investment in a healthy environment for our children, directing my food dollars toward organic farmers is part of my spiritual practice. Simply put, we choose to support an agricultural system that does not rely on toxic chemicals to produce the food we eat."

Broccoli Robbed

Think you're looking at broccoli when browsing your local supermarket produce section? Well, it looks like broccoli and it walks like broccoli and it talks like broccoli, but it ain't broccoli. It's broccoli robbed...robbed of its value, its quality, its health-giving benefits, its meaning. It's a phony.

The meaning of broccoli, its virtue, is to give us health. Broccoli is not about taste for most people — we add butter or cheese or put it in or with something else to give it some taste. It is not a comfort food. If you eat it raw, you needn't stop at the gas station. Broccoli is not about good looks either. It looks like a fat, ugly, overpruned tree for a model railroad town. Broccoli exists only to give us health.

It seems very odd, then, that although broccoli is one of the most resistant vegetables to insect attacks, it may have been sprayed with up to seventeen different poisons, some of which are inside it and can't be washed off. It's been fed chemical fertilizers that may contain recycled toxic wastes. Nine metals found in fertilizers, like arsenic and lead, are known or suspected to cause cancer, and metals like mercury are linked to developmental defects. And broccoli is one of the least contaminated crops we have.

By the time the broccoli gets to our supermarket, any connection to the farm it was grown on and the corporation that grew it has been lost. Who knows where it's from or how it was treated or what is in and on it? But when we get it home, it still has some beneficial cancer-fighting, heart disease–fighting antioxidant flavonoids left. So we pop it in the microwave, which then destroys 97 percent of the antioxidants, or we boil it, which destroys 66 percent of the antioxidants. (Steaming it destroys less than 10 percent.) If it wasn't for shelf life, it "wouldn't have no life at all."

But my organic broccoli is full of meaning. Raised by the Decater family up in Covelo, California (see chapter 7), this broccoli is delivered every week to a home in town where families enrolled in the farm's annual program meet to pick it up. Gloria Decater unloads the truck with one of her sons, chatting away about what's going on at the farm and what's included in this week's basket. I ask her how the broccoli is this week, and she says that the caterpillars from the cabbage white butterfly are the exact same color as the broccoli stalk, almost impossible to see, but they haven't had a problem with them this year because they planted some dill and other companion herbs to distract them from the broccoli. Some aphids appeared, but they were washed off with the hose.

My broccoli is beautiful and vibrant and full of meaning. It's meaningful to me that Stephen and Gloria care enough about me and their farm and their family to not have poisons around. It means more work, but that's the trade-off. It's meaningful that Gloria and Stephen take the time to explain why the food is healthy and good in the newsletter they enclose with the basket. It's meaningful that the person who grew the food also brought it in to town and handed it to me in a basket with a big smile. She's proud to offer it, and I'm grateful not just to her, but *for* her and *for* Stephen. I've been on their farm, I know who they are. It's not that I appreciate only that they are providers, that they are just utilitarian and of use to the community. That would be merely self-serving. Their dignity and worth lie in their character and in their humanity and in the love they bring to everything they do. That is quality that cannot be measured. That is meaning in and of itself, and my honor is in being part of a community that includes them. And that is about as close to truth and beauty and gratitude as I can get.

Nell and Peter

She is the daughter of a famous actor and actress. He owned the successful pool cleaning business that took care of her family's pool. They were friendly and liked each other. She moved to the West Coast to attend college and they lost contact. He sold his pool cleaning business and moved to the West Coast to pursue other opportunities. An avid falconer, she learned that these powerful birds of prey could soon become extinct because of DDT use. She had herself tested and found dozens of toxic poisons in her own body and became a believer in organic foods.

One day, listening to a fund-raising appeal on the local public radio station while driving down the freeway near her home, she heard them announce the name of a new donor, Peter Meehan. "Peter!" she shouted to herself. It was synchronicity. Her old pool cleaning friend, Peter Meehan, was living within miles of Nell, unbeknownst to either of them, and he was a businessman who had been looking for just the right business to be involved in.

Nell had talked about organic food with her dad, who owned a food company whose profits all went to charity. But he had been introduced to "health foods" before and had not enjoyed the experience (could it have been the gravy made from brewer's yeast?). So now she decided to test him again. She cooked up the now-famous Thanksgiving meal for the family and afterward asked her dad how he liked it. He said it was the best Thanksgiving meal they'd ever had. She told him it was all organic, and that she wanted to start an organic branch of his food business to raise money for organic agriculture. He told her to go do the research, but his favorite snack food being pretzels, he "didn't want one that tastes like a dog bone."

Nell Newman and Peter Meehan did the research, and Paul Newman gave it the go-ahead. Newman's Own Organics was born. Cofounder and CEO Peter Meehan had found "just the right business" and the perfect partner. There was one last hitch. Paul Newman told them that they could do their own business using the Newman brand, but they didn't have to give the profits to charity like he was doing. Nell stood up and said: "Oh, that's just great, Dad. We'll be the division that keeps the money! We wouldn't even consider that." Giving the money to causes was what excited both of them. "Do you really mean that?" Paul asked. They did. All profits, now in the millions, go into funding organic research, and the popularity of the brand has brought success not only to the company but to the many small organic farms that supply it.

There's a saying that synchronicity happens when God wants to remain anonymous. Whatever the mysterious cause and effect may be, synchronicity is a nudge indicating that we have aligned ourselves with something of greater purpose. What could possibly be a more meaningful business? And with corruption running so rampant and the greedy so shamelessly grinning from the covers of our business magazines, here's a suggestion for new models for business executives: President Nell Newman and CEO Peter Meehan.

Network of Renegades

May I introduce you to my community in a little more detail? Not because my community is special, or chock-full of heroes, or somehow exemplary in its community involvement, or because I want to put the heroes I see around me on a pedestal. Somewhat like Garrison Keillor's fictional community of Lake Wobegon, my corner of the world is both unique and typical; it's unique in the characters that abound unlike anywhere else, and it's typical because every community is typically unlike any other. My community just happens to be one that I know, and its heroes are typical of the diversity of characters one can find anywhere.

Mendocino County is located about two hours north of the Golden Gate Bridge. I won't belabor you with a tourist pamphlet's description of what this community offers in recreational opportunities or the Chamber of Commerce descriptions of industrial job patterns. Mendocino County features picturesque vineyards, including a thriving organic wine industry. We have some redwood forests that are not yet logged off, as well as hidden marijuana plantations. We have our right wing and our left wing. We have our Green Party and our skinheads. We have a minority population who does the real work, and we have trust-funders who have time to monkey around with non-profit do-gooder issues. We have a couple of alternative newspapers, and one paper owned by some remote conglomerate. Ukiah is fairly progressive politically, with a city council that voted against the Iraq War, and developers who want very much to grow the town up the hills and into the woods. It's typical. It's unique.

I've lived in Northern California over the past forty years and in the wine/redwood country of Sonoma and Mendocino Counties for the past twenty. We have a lot of very sincere, hardworking political and environmental activists in our community. This is where Judi Bari famously led the fight to save the redwoods. (She was blown up by a pipe bomb in nearby Oakland.) We also have our share of pseudoactivists who are outraged at right-wing sins and radically incisive in their analysis and intellectual solutions but do little to change things. In practice, the bucolic surroundings and easy access to high-quality "bud" (marijuana) often temper angry temperaments into long, laid-back, extemporaneous condemnations of our nation's plight, eager verbal support of taking on the bad guys, and another weekend of walks in the woods and visits to the beach. But here and there, just like where you live, are some true heroes.

Courage in Action

Allen and Els Cooperrider missed their kids. To bring the family back together, they started a business, the Ukiah Brewing Company, with a total investment of $400,000 and current annual sales of $900,000. Els made history and news worldwide when she decided to take on the chemical MegaMaws, worth billions, with the help of a community gathered around their tiny business in this remote small town.

Els Cooperrider grew up in a Holland devastated by a world war and German occupation, everyone struggling to get back on their feet, dealing with neighbors' lost families and concentration camp horror stories. A deep sense of injustice was bred by the nonstop stories of woe all around her, and that burden established a personal value system that when faced with a choice between confronting something wrong and unjust or ignoring it, she could not help but stand up to the challenge, come what may. And she paid dearly for it.

After immigrating with her family to the United States, Els received a bachelor's degree in botany from the University of California, Berkeley, and a master's degree in range science.

"I had always worked in laboratories and had a job at Colorado State University School of Veterinary Medicine in Fort Collins, Colorado," Els says.

I had been in charge of the lab for five years, when a postdoctoral fellow who had just joined the university began bringing in contraband radioactive materials, [including] an isotope called tritium, which is a gas that the H-bomb is made from. He was using it to mark DNA, but our lab was not licensed to use radioactive materials. Tritium is a beta emitter, and the main health effect from radiation is cancer. You have to be extremely careful with it, and labs that have licenses to use it have to keep pregnant women completely away from it. This postdoc fellow was being irresponsible by not letting me know what he was working with or keeping any scientific records in the lab about what he was doing, and we had a pregnant woman on our staff. When I discovered what was going on, I was faced with a decision that would change my life if I blew the whistle, or I could simply ignore it and stay safe. I blew the whistle.

When I confronted the postdoc fellow, he became enraged and started calling me names, then picked up a bag with this tritium in it, opened it, and threw it in my face. I was flabbergasted. I went to the professor in charge and he said not to say anything, that I'd be just fine. I then went to the radiation control office, filed a grievance, and that got me fired. Fifteen months later I had cancer (which eventually required seventeen operations), and I took them to court. The first trial resulted in a mistrial, and in the second trial, the main witness to the incident, a graduate student, had mysteriously disappeared and I lost the case. During the trial the Colorado attorney general asked the jury not to award me any money because I was dying anyway and the state couldn't afford it!

After I was fired, I applied for 85 different positions and couldn't get one job, not even for four dollars an hour cleaning foxtails out of cats' paws. We were out of money, our two boys were grown and on their own, so we came back to California to live in this small cabin in the woods in Mendocino County that was in Allen's family — along a creek, off the grid, no phone service, miles from the nearest small town, Ukiah.

I began involving myself in local politics and environmental matters and led an effort to ban roadside pesticide spraying in the county. We took on the State Department of Transportation and are now the only county in California where both the county and state mows its weeds along roads rather than killing them with toxic chemicals.

We missed our sons, Bret and Sid, who we'd left behind in Colorado, so I started scheming on how to get them here. You aren't supposed to leave your sons; they are supposed to move away from you! Bret was a brewer and wanted to start his own brewery. So we helped raise investment funds from family, community, and small business loans. I insisted that the beer and food we served had to be organic, which hadn't been done before in the country — one, for the environment, and everything that entails; two, it's better for the workers in the field who have to grow all this stuff; and three, it's better for the people who eat and drink. I would not have been involved if we weren't going to be organic. I couldn't work in a place that served up food and beer with poisons in them. At the time, there was one certified organic restaurant, in Washington, D.C., and no organic breweries. Bret could find organic hops, but only one kind of organic barley, so he would be confined to making one beer *only. Later, more organic grains became available, and we now provide a good selection.*

I had no idea how hard it would be to find organic food and have it delivered to us in food service sizes at reasonable prices. We have to buy organic feta cheese in eight-ounce packages. The other difficulty is that, instead of getting delivery from one truck, four times a week, we get it from fifty-two different purveyors of produce, cheese, eggs, olives, and meats. All of our beef is organic and grass-fed. Most beef is finished off with corn the last few weeks, but grass-fed beef get little or no grain, and don't get as fat. And the fat is not nearly as saturated. It has oily, yellow fat, not white, hard, and dry fat like grain-fed beef. The composition of grass-fed fat is the same as fish, high in omega-3s, much healthier for you. We buy as much from local and regional organic farmers as possible. We get very fresh, wild, sustainably harvested, non-GMO fish from our coast here, and we buy all of our wines within Mendocino County. We are the first certified organic brewpub, and the second certified organic restaurant in the country.

The idea here is to make a living, not a killing. We want to provide good organic food at a reasonable, affordable price. We talked about a place that would be a social center, but we didn't think it would actually happen the way it has. It took about three years for it to become an unofficial town hall. Three vital community organizations were founded and grew at the brewery — the Mendocino Organic Network and its Mendocino Renegade label, GMO Free Mendocino, which came out of the Organic Network, and the local alternative newspaper, The Bullhorn, *all got started here.*

I'm a cofounder of Mendocino Organic Network, which is a small group of volunteers that offer certification services for small, local, organic farmers. [The author is also a cofounder.] The conventional certification services that are now available have all been compromised by the government's involvement. They used to have stricter standards until the USDA took it over, and now they are being watered down. We decided to come up with our own program of certifying farmers with the original organic standards that give the consumer what we think is healthier, safer food. A lot of the small, local, organic market farmers could not afford the increasing fees of the USDA certification, and the amount of paperwork required was also prohibitive to small farmers. So our label, which we call Mendocino Renegade, stands for better standards and support of local farmers, and the fees are about 20 percent of what they had to pay before. We are all volunteer, with certification done by other local organic farmers, by their peers.

MegaMaw Meets Earth Mother

During a meeting of the Mendocino Organic Network, I suggested that we try and ban genetically modified organisms (GMOs) from the county. As a biologist, having taken genetics and having studied biology for all these years, I realized that people are picking apart the very essence of life and reorganizing it as if they were God; it is something so preposterous I can't handle it. They're man-made organisms. It's horrible. Not because I have a religious belief about it, but just think, in order for an organism such as ourselves to be here, it has required 3 million years and random mutations and natural selection to get to this final product which is us, or a soybean, or corn. Then people just decided to start playing with those genetics as if those millions of years were for naught. It is bad thinking, shortsighted, and it's going to cause havoc. We haven't seen the end of it yet. We're talking about crop failures, infestations, superweeds — but we really haven't seen what these organisms are going to do. I love this community, and the potential negative consequences to it and to our personal and collective health affront our dignity. Democratically, polls show an overwhelming citizen demand that GMOs be at least labeled on our food, yet the biotech industry refuses to comply.

The Precautionary Principle says that if you can prove that it will do no harm, then maybe go ahead. But proving something is not going to do any harm is very difficult to do. So the Precautionary Principle is really: If in doubt, don't do it. But that principle doesn't exist anywhere in America. Realizing that a cornstalk is not real makes me think of The Invasion of the Body Snatchers. We and the corn didn't co-evolve. That corn is not real. Our gut has never dealt with the proteins in that plant and has no way to deal with them.

Monkeys given a bioengineered banana and a natural banana will eat the natural banana. Who knows what the repercussions will be in the insect world, with earthworms and microbes. This is a big experiment that is driven by money and greed, with no look at the consequences.

So I proposed that we write up an ordinance to ban GMO crops from our county, and then either have the board of supervisors vote it in or collect signatures and put it on the ballot. We well knew that we could be taking on the biggest, baddest, multinational corporations around with countless billions of dollars at their disposal, but we didn't know if they would actually come into the county and try to stop us. They did.

But Mendocino County voters defeated the world's largest producers of genetically engineered foods and seed, which pumped a record $621,000 into a county of 47,000 voters. Monsanto, DuPont, Dow Chemical, and a consortium of other biotech multinational corporations shattered spending records in our small agricultural county, but they were no match for thousands of Mendocino County farmers, business owners, vintners, and families who joined the largest, most successful grassroots campaign the county has ever seen to fight the encroachment of genetically altered crops.

We're the first county in the U.S. to prohibit the growing of genetically altered crops and animals — but we won't be the last. Our success has already inspired nine other California counties to enact similar measures. We proved that no amount of money can replace the love and commitment of people who care passionately about the place they live. This is a turning point in the corporate domination of the food system and a reclaiming of responsibility for agriculture at a local level.

They had the money, we had the people.

A mom and dad, their two sons, a few hundred thousand investment dollars, a safe place, and inspiration for a community to take on the MegaMaws and beat them. This is the promise of a democratic society fulfilled.

Values Build Character

If you are looking for courage, character, and wisdom, find someone who lives a wise life. If you're looking for truth, find someone who lives truthfully. Find a philosopher of the soil whose wisdom and meaning come from producing that which *is* life and which *nurtures* life. And instead of asking them questions and probing for articulate and deep reflections, simply observe. Spend some time with your Creative Action Heroes; work with them in their daily tasks; be of use to them in the same way that they are of use to the world around them. Like Jesus' advice that "by their fruits ye will know them," look first to those who lovingly coax fruits and vegetables from the earth, because it is from the earth that all life comes. And, for me, the most deeply wise and knowing are those who live from the earth. They also can be cranky, cantankerous, and eccentric, adding to our great diversity of life and character.

Much of their truth comes from the fact that they have courageously figured out a way to live fairly independently and can therefore speak the truth without fear. If you know how to feed yourself and your family directly from the soil, you live with less fear. And with less fear comes more truth.

Before we can move much further with courage and confidence to make the many positive changes crying for creative action, we have to stop the poisoning and the cancers being caused by an agricultural system that puts mammon before man, dollars before people. We gotta get our food right. It's killing us.

Courage

Vandana Shiva is a physicist and philosopher of science who gave up a successful career to become deeply engaged in the ecological, social, and economic struggles of subsistence workers in India. She has stood beside people in their struggles against destructive forestry practices, large-scale dams, and multinational-dominated agribusiness.

Her recent work, as director of the Research Foundation for Science, Technology, and Natural Resource Policy in Dehra Dun, India, has concentrated largely on protecting farmers' rights to their own seed stock and exposing the threats to the world's farmers by the potent combination of global liberalization of trade and patent protection of agricultural processes and products.

Shiva has been a global advocate for the legal and commercial rights of traditional farmers (a majority of them women) who have over the centuries developed plant and animal breeds for their resistance to pests and climatic extremes, their superior flavor and nutritional value, and their appropriateness to local farming and cultural requirements. She writes:

Organic agriculture to me is the movement for peace, the deepest movement for peace, because it creates peace at that fundamental level where it rests on ecological security, creates economic and political and social security, and therefore doesn't have any place for wars and violence and arms. But there is another dimension to peacemaking through organic agriculture that it is by its very nature democratic. You cannot be an organic farmer and have Monsanto tell you exactly what to do: The earth tells you what to do. You cannot be an organic producer and not have relationships of a decentralized economy. It is that decentralized economy that creates conditions of peace.

The virtue of courage may be best realized with the freedom and independence of mind and spirit that follow the Jeffersonian ideals of a just, agrarian society based on individual self-sufficiency and decentralized institutions. But now with the exploding globalization of communication and trade, population growth crowding the planet, including our own continent, and pollution degrading the global atmosphere, we can no longer escape the consequences of everyone else's lifestyle. We are all connected, and it is now the local community, whether urban or rural, with a regionalized agrarian support system, that seems a more suitable ideal. As inevitably rising energy prices affect the energy-intensive costs of food — the cost of transportation, chemical fertilizers, and chemical pesticides — it will be the labor-intensive local, small, organic farms that will once again become the key support of community life. And the skill of small organic farmers will become most meaningful to every local community.

Meaningful work comes alive
when purposeful courage fits community needs.
And that requires love....

CHAPTER SEVEN

love

[useful you]

We have not even to risk the adventure alone; for the heroes of all time have gone before us; the labyrinth is thoroughly known; we have only to follow the thread of the hero-path. And where we had thought to find an abomination, we shall find a god; where we had thought to slay another, we shall slay ourselves; where we had thought to travel outward, we shall come to the center of our own existence; where we had thought to be alone, we shall be with all the world.

— Joseph Campbell

It is when you are really living in the present — working, thinking, lost, absorbed in something you care about very much, that you are living spiritually. . . . For I know that the energy of the creative impulse comes from love and all its manifestations — admiration, compassion, glowing respect, gratitude, praise, tenderness, adoration, enthusiasm. And why should we all use our creative power? Because there is nothing that makes people so generous, joyful, lively, bold, and compassionate.

— Brenda Ueland

Say nothing of my religion. It is known to God and myself alone. Its evidence before the world is to be sought in my life: if it has been honest and dutiful to society the religion which has regulated it cannot be a bad one.

— Thomas Jefferson

I wonder if you've found useful work that stretches you, that you find meaningful, that requires your passion and deep commitment, and also allows a decent standard of living. In times like these, there is so much that needs doing, fixing, caring, yet what pays well is often frivolous or deadly boring. When I become especially alarmed about the environmental issues we face, as is easy for someone raised on end-times eschatology, I ponder the experiences of my generation with living simply and working cooperatively. Were we forecasting and practicing for the approaching need for a more sustainable living and a more equitable distribution of resources? Whether oil is about to run out, or to get very expensive, or to destroy us with global warming, big changes are necessary and coming, whether next week, next year, or ten years from now. Our food is extraordinarily dependent on oil to fertilize, grow, harvest, process, and transport to us. Prudence and responsibility suggest making changes now, rather than later, in an emergency, when our choices have narrowed considerably. Prudence suggests becoming more self-sufficient in our local communities. Whatever the future holds for us all, we cannot continue to waste and pollute and squander as we have.

I recall a president who mounted solar panels on the roof of the White House as a practical, responsible symbol of prudent long-term planning. I also recall another president in a postelection hissy fit tearing them off in an irresponsible one-finger salute from the Mega-Maws. This path not taken could come to haunt us.

In a time of growing evidence that a crisis is at hand, lack of temperance and prudence is nothing other than a self-centered lack of love and responsibility for others. It's the teenaged, greasy-haired rebel without a cause showing off his macho bravado, foot jammed on the throttle, Elvis blasting, cigarette dangling, knuckles dragging, head nonchalantly tilted in utter abandonment to the ego, playing chicken with the universe. There's a police photo of him still on the wall down at the highway patrol, draped over the door of his crushed hot rod, with the caption: "He was cool. He went fast." It doesn't say how many he took with him.

Thankfully, all is not doom and gloom. Opportunity beckons for those flexible enough to grow and change and meet challenges with creativity and optimism.

Future Skills

History records Confucius as first stating the Golden Rule, so loving our neighbors has always been considered a virtue by the wisdom traditions. The teachings of Jesus went further, making love the *principal* virtue, the supreme law of human life, upon which all of our daily acts should be based, and extending it even to our enemies and to those with other belief systems. He taught us to avoid resisting those who are evil, and he said that if someone steals something of yours, give them something else of yours also. There is no reason or excuse to use violence against another. This may seem an impossible philosophy these days, but once an exception is allowed, then a second and a third can be allowed, and the advice becomes meaningless.

Leo Tolstoy explained this teaching and helped influence another, Mohandas Gandhi, who lived and practiced it socially and politically. "Love-force," the political application of nonviolence, was powerfully demonstrated by this skinny little man who had been treated unfairly, who recognized the systemic injustice that his treatment revealed, and who led the toppling of the reigning superpower, an empire so vast they said the sun never set on it. The soul-force of active love is powerful beyond imagining.

Nonviolence is often misunderstood as cringing, fearful, peace-at-all-costs, do-nothing, naive cowardice. But properly applied, nonviolent political action is a powerful tool for change, and requires the bravest, most resolute of personalities. Nonviolent action led by Gandhi, Martin Luther King Jr., and Cesar Chavez brought victory over entrenched power, and there are also others, less well-known examples. In the 1950s dictators were toppled in Guatemala and Honduras by nonviolent means, as well as Philippine dictator Ferdinand Marcos in 1986. Illegitimate authority requires our support and acquiescence to endure. When we withdraw them, power becomes powerless. Whether we withdraw our support by boycotting grapes, refusing genetically engineered plants in our communities, refusing to sit in the back of the bus, or refusing to buy salt when it's readily available for free, as Gandhi did with his Salt March — whenever we start doing what is in our interests, and stop doing what is in theirs, the rule of illegitimate authority crumbles to nothing. Especially in a democracy, such withdrawal of support, along with the willingness to suffer any consequences rather than make others suffer, is the power of love in action.

Our neighbors are now the whole world, and loving our neighbors means something much greater than it ever has. We can choose a different mode of existence, one that empathizes and cares for others, that includes all in our conceptual community, that shares more and regards cooperation and mutuality as the prime values of democratic inclusion.

The skills that are going to matter most in the near future will no longer be just the technical, logical, left-brain skills that have given us commodities galore. We are now completely overshooting our wants, pouring endless streams of meaningless, needless junk into our garages, attics, storage spaces, and landfills, made by who knows who, who knows where. Those skills are now being outsourced, and we need to figure out what skills are needed now. And it doesn't take a rocket scientist. The right-brain skills of empathy, community, cooperation, and caring are now required. What the world needs now is some of that good, good lovin'. Creative, active love in action.

What Am I Doing Here?

Our culture has been extremely adept at obscuring and concealing the fact of personal death. In one of Tolstoy's most famous novellas, *The Death of Ivan Ilyich*, a respected judge faces the end of his life. He realizes that the gnawing pain in his side is going to kill him. He's done all the right things, played all the social games, known all the right people, had a respected career. Now he goes through the stages of denial, fear, and anger at his friends and family, and he begins to realize what he has lost and ignored as he climbed the social and professional ladder. As death draws near and he resigns himself to it, he realizes the meaning of life, which is all the love he missed and ignored.

The story does not reveal any great new truth or guidance or secret of life's meaning. Instead, whenever I read it, I'm faced with taking a review of my own life, the choices I've made that have placed me here now, and the effect of those choices on loved ones and others I've met along the way. Sure there are regrets, and things I'd do differently, and choices I'd have changed in retrospect. But most of all, the story presents me with what I will do tonight, and tomorrow. And it causes a great wonderment at what all the fussing and fighting and getting and accumulating are about.

We still have a chance to get it right if we start now. There apparently is still time (although some say it's too late). We still have a chance to retrace our steps, now grown faint in the sand, find the fork we left behind, and take the road we abandoned earlier. Along with the necessary actions against what is going wrong, active love that cares about others requires positive actions that build the future for those who will live in it. It will take the full-on, fully funded support of a sustainable society built on renewable resources. It will require millions of us doing useful, meaningful work. It will mean a mass transfer of funds from world military dominance to building a peaceful infrastructure. Plans have already been proposed; it will take all of us to implement them. The billions of dollars now used to destroy can be turned elsewhere to create a bountiful, sustainable future. (See www.apolloalliance.org for one example.) But the MegaMaws will have to be tamed, the dominance outgrown, the hierarchies tempered, and grassroots democracies created. It will take no less than all hands on deck in a full and loving rush to the future...starting now.

Doris "Granny D." Haddock, at the age of eighty-nine, walked across the country to demonstrate her concern about how our nation's leaders have been corrupted by special interest dollars and no longer represent the interests of their neighbors and constituents. She walked ten miles daily for fourteen months, making speeches along the way. Later, in her ninety-third birthday speech, she said, "Aren't we privileged to live in a time when everything is at stake, and when our efforts make a difference in the eternal contest between the forces of light and shadow, between togetherness and division? Between justice and exploitation? Oh, be joyful that you are a warrior in this great time! Will we rise to this battle? If so, we cannot lose, for rising up to it is our victory. If we represent love in the world, you see, we have already won."

Abstracted Work

I've come to believe that one reason our culture is adrift is that we've lost our direct connections with each other through, among other things, our daily work. Each step of greater abstraction, greater size, greater distance, is a step away from meaning, and a loss of values. Each step in growing larger — size of company, size of government, size of institution — results in each job becoming more specialized, more abstracted, and less meaningful. Each step that expands the distance between family members, between company offices — whether within a building or within a country — or the number of miles a food item travels on the way to market results in another level of meaning being eroded away. In this Darwinian business world, impatience to grow fast and grow big results in loss of meaning.

Thus, greater abstraction, distance, and size result in a loss of direct connection between people. As that connection diminishes, so too does meaning diminish. And as we lose connections and meaning, we lose our values, because values are supported by these human connections. If I'm a corporate farmer in California growing food that will be sold to consumers in Ohio, the "others" that I am "doing unto" are little more than an abstraction in my mind. I'll never meet them. And it's quite unlikely they will ever do a thing back unto me, good or bad, because they have no idea who I am or how I'm connected with their food. They may have "demographic significance" for my advertising agency, but beyond that I don't think about them as individuals, only as a mass. So if I put poisons in their food in order to eradicate a pest in my fields more cheaply and easily, what's the big deal? I will have no knowledge of them, and thus no sense of connection with them, however my action affects their personal health, and they will have no knowledge of or connection to the decisions I personally made that affected them. The Golden Rule does not work between demographic profiles or abstractions — only between real people connected directly as neighbors, friends, and coworkers, or in direct community trade relationships. Abstractions remove responsibility.

Adam Smith, author of *The Wealth of Nations* and often thought of as the father of modern economics, launched the economic doctrine of free enterprise and the free market — now a political religion — as well as the idea of "the invisible hand," which theorizes that if each person makes decisions based on personal self-interest, then the overall economy will work most efficiently for the happiness of all. This is interpreted by many to mean anything goes, greed is good, every person for themselves. But that wasn't all that Smith said. He also said that for free enterprise to work, there must be widespread adherence to morality; he said that the purpose of government is to defend the poor from the rich, and he opposed corporations that involve absentee control because it weakens connection, and therefore diminishes responsibility.

The ultimate abstraction is the financial spreadsheet, which gives no indication that every change of every number is affecting someone somewhere, positively or negatively. As the company vice president moves that number from this cell to that cell, a thousand invisible people, gathered to watch over his shoulders, cheer or groan. Grumbling is heard, shoulders are gently rubbed, tears softly shed. People's lives are hanging in the balance as the VP pauses at the keyboard, covering a yawn. Who will take responsibility for those lives? The autonomy and dignity of a thousand human beings have just been smothered as the computer is turned off and another boring day at the office comes to an end. He was just doing the job he learned so well in college. The CEO was just growing his investors' capital. The investor was just trying to find a company that would give him the best return on his investment. Who will take responsibility?

Changing Values

We can take great comfort in knowing that our values can change over time, adapt to a changing world, and evolve progressively as we grow in wisdom through knowledge and experience. The Golden Rule may be an unchanging maxim, but its application in time and place and circumstance can thankfully be adapted.

Examples of such adaptation show that it's not an easy process. It requires an insightful honesty that challenges the status quo. For instance, millions were burned at the stake because they were considered religious heretics. Love in action challenged the religious authorities and dismissed their way of forcing agreement on others, and we've grown into wiser values. Heretics are good. Differences of opinion challenge our beliefs, add to our diversity, and help us change and grow.

Millions were enslaved and owned by others. Love in action challenged the status quo, and we've grown into wiser values. Slavery was wrong, and facing it down made us change and grow. Millions were denied the vote in our democracy because of gender oppression. Love in action challenged the denial of suffrage as illegitimate, and we've grown into wiser values. Women are equal, and acknowledging this continues to make us change and grow.

Thirty-some-odd years ago, love in action challenged the power structure that insisted that we had to bomb and poison millions into oblivion in a war based on lies. We protested and withdrew our support and the leaders responsible whimpered away into their own oblivions, and we've grown into wiser values.

The Golden Rule, and a democratic society, cannot operate without honesty. Love in action will always challenge the decisions and consequences of dishonesty — personally, politically, and culturally. Love in action has challenged the culture of fear and death that walks with greed and injustice and authority and fixed truth, and love in action has withdrawn its support. Love in action grows into wiser, ever changing, always progressing values. Anything and everything is possible when imagination is set free from fear, the opposite of love. The higher authority is love, and it lives in every heart.

Love in Action

Love refuses to dominate. Love nurtures, cultivates, communicates, and cooperates, which requires emotional connection, feelings, sensitivity, and relationship. Unfortunately, in our culture these values are not often associated with the masculine. We men have been raised to value power, command, control, and violence, and to shut off the wide range of emotional connections we fear would emasculate us. We are raised to take charge, to be responsible; we work hard, we provide. But to create men — ready to defend, to impose our will, to go to war ready to die and to kill — our culture glorifies the action hero who is aloof, cut off, separate, heavily armed, dominant.

Here again we can look to the organic farmer as a better model. Particularly we men can look to organic farming men and women, who have learned nurturing values by working with nature. Their work is life enhancing, connected, emotionally rewarded. Their values and their ability to love and nurture are the values of the future if we are to survive. You can meet them, learn from them — they're there every weekend in their stalls at the farmers' market. They're no different, really. They are struggling to survive like we all are, mul-titasking, juggling priorities and details, worried about a daughter's first date and a son's making the team, but there is sense of indepen-dence, of self-esteem, of being equal to life's challenges that a life out of doors, connected with fundamentals, gives the organic farmer.

The Decater family runs a CSA (community-supported agricul-ture) and partially solar-powered farm that every week supplies its 180 member families in Mendocino County and the Bay Area with fresh, high-quality biodynamic/organic food. They plow and till the land with their four draft horses. Besides growing almost fifty vari-eties of vegetables, they raise sheep, cows, chickens, and pigs.

We sit on old wooden chairs in the flower garden as the after-noon sun passes its zenith and heads toward the Pacific, miles west of us. Gloria has been flitting around the farm on a bike with a class of third graders from Marin County. Camped out for four days of hard labor, they are absorbed in various projects organized by sev-eral farm apprentices and parents. Stephen has been out around the barn and pastures, working with apprentices who are planting and harvesting greens. Gloria has on old Levi's and sandals with heavy wool socks; Stephen is in a worn green plaid flannel shirt, heavily soiled Levi's, and deeply scuffed work boots. Despite their long hours and heavy schedules, they're relaxed. They begin by describ-ing the beauty and love they found in a garden....

STEPHEN: *I met Alan Chadwick [see chapter 2] in 1967 at his garden project at the University of California, Santa Cruz. As a young, idealis-tic person I saw Alan as an older person doing something that was totally positive for the world ... and this was during the Vietnam War with all kinds of awful things happening around us. The adage of beating your swords into plowshares felt real when I was putting my energy in that direction, growing food and flowers. Working in the garden opened this whole world of beauty and culture: the history of different flowers, where they had come from, how they needed to be taken care of, this whole world of activity, with the human being in nature, working in a supportive way.*

That took my heart and interest and eventually became what I spent all my time doing.

The garden was so vitally alive, and we were immersed in that life. When you are with the flowers for a couple of hours morning after morning, they have a kind of soul expression of the Earth, an expression of love. In Alan's creation of a garden for people to come into and be immersed in, he was actually trying to create a healing. Those were "back-to-the-land" times, when people were wanting to reconnect with nature. Alan was doing that in a very conscious and cultured way. It wasn't "go back to nature by going wild" but rather, go to nature by recognizing the life there and working with the cultural skills that have been humankind's heredity for centuries. For me it was the raw life-force connection, but at the same time, it was the cultural and artistic beauty a human being could create in the world as opposed to the ways humans destroy life.

So I've been trying to create the garden in my own life ever since then, and create it as a garden that is open to people so they have contact with nature, see it, feel it. You can talk about experiencing nature forever, but when someone comes in and their nose is immersed in a living flower, it suddenly hits them with the true expression of life. You are meeting other "beings," not just human beings. It's like when you are in relationship with someone and feel the love and caring that comes from them . . . that is something that is real and has an impact on your spirit and heart. In the garden you experience nature as being alive.

I followed Alan here to the Covelo Garden Project, where Gloria and I met, and we eventually began running our own farm. Everything in nature serves something else: the earth serves the plants, the fruit of the plants serves the animals, the manure from the animals serves the earth. [A screeching "cockadoodle" rings out from the barn area.] We can learn those relationships by becoming part of them. It was critical back in Santa Cruz. . . . I was bringing my friends into the garden there, and it continues to be critical in this urban-separated world to experience the bounty of food as a Gift.

When we talk with the kids who visit us, we ask them, "Where did this farm come from? Where did the animals come from? Did we make *any of those things?" These things come from the wild world, nature, creation, to begin with, but when we bring them into the farm, we begin to culture them. You don't have a farm without a human being. Without the human being, Mother Nature is taking care of the culture. So on the farm, we are being cocreative with nature, and we experience that relationship. Even though most people are not living on farms today, we are still eating food from farms that are occupying land somewhere. The problem is that now it's an anonymous relationship. But in order to have real appreciation for the gifts of nature, our relationships with those gifts need to be more conscious. People eating food need to recognize that their partners are the Earth and the people growing the food — not some factory somewhere.*

GLORIA: *Our school classes, which include parents, are here from the Bay Area for four days, and they only fully "arrive" on the farm about the second morning. They may not be able to verbalize their experience necessarily, but at some point in time, for some people immediately and for others after they leave, even ten or fifteen years later, they look back and say, "That was the first time I really experienced life, living, the gift of life" — and they're grateful for it. I've heard that from so many. That's why we continue to share this farm. If I couldn't feel that, and if there wasn't that appreciation, I couldn't do it. But I see the impact. [We can hear one of the Decater sons, Nicholas, pounding nails nearby as he finishes his current tool shop building project.] I've heard from quite a few college kids in their twenties who came here in third grade; they say it was the most intense experience in their school education, and they remember everything. When they come as kids, they can be, and succeed, and thrive on the farm in a way they can't in school — and it can change their relationship with their classmates and teachers. The work they do here is not something made up for them. It's real, valuable work that helps the farm go forward. It has an impact. They can feel it. They develop a sense of worth that they didn't have before. And parents, realizing that their spoiled children are very capable of doing things if they'll just let them, say: "Oh, they can be responsible! Oh, we've spoiled them rotten. We'd better change that. The way we're raising them isn't right."*

STEPHEN: *Out of that they can see that shoveling up that manure to make compost is something human beings have devoted their lives to for thousands of years. [As Stephen begins to ruminate, Gloria moves nearby for some spontaneous weeding.] I once had an experience where I was totally distraught, worrying about different things, and I couldn't really work, and finally in frustration I went out and started shoveling manure. All of a sudden it was like hundreds of thousands of people from centuries back in time were standing right there beside me, and I was shoveling manure with them as they had been doing for thousands of years. And it was like, "Okay! I'm not alone. I can do this!" This is where life is at, doing these mundane tasks, but they're not separated out of time — they're continuous with the whole of human experience. Our modern world separates us from that connection and that relationship. And the beauty of farming is this universality of life and activity that is flowing through the whole world. When we become part of that we lose our alienation and our separation; we can come together and recognize our relationships.*

GLORIA [returning to the group]: *A farmer's life is so rhythmical, and that is why farmers can continue to work on and on through the days and years. When you're doing something in rhythm it's so much less tiring. For example, scything grain is really a dance form, and when you get going it is so beautiful, so enjoyable. You think to yourself how farmers in the past would get together and scythe all day, and sing, and be joyful, and how they loved it. When you milk a cow, you're milking two teats at once. If you milk only one teat, you are twice as tired than if you milk two teats at once in rhythm. There's just no comparison. That rhythm is so joyful.*

STEPHEN: *Hard, physical work can be enjoyable and rewarding. The bad rap in agriculture has come because people worked so hard and still couldn't make a living — they weren't economically compensated for their work. Eliminating people from agriculture has disconnected us all from the soil and the land. A farmer has two tasks: growing food that is nourishing is one level, but on another level there is a spiritual nourishment that comes only from being in a farm and experiencing the work of a farm. We need farms that can create that opportunity. Even if we could produce all of our food with corporate industrial organic production, although it would be better for the environment than conventional farming with chemicals, it would still leave people largely out of agriculture — we would still not have a culturally or socially conscious agriculture. If it's going through a regular market system, there is a disconnect with people using that food, knowing where it comes from, how it is grown, whether the farmer's needs are being met, and if the growing methods are sustainable long-term. This is cultural nourishment and spiritual nourishment that people are missing out on. [An apprentice stops by to ask advice about the harness they will be putting on the draft horses for the afternoon plowing.]*

We need a new kind of farm, one that is not only market-oriented, as simply a producing unit, but a farm that is also an oasis that people can come into and experience the culture of their agriculture. It is too fundamental a part of human life to be left out of one's existence. Large machinery and monocropping block that potential. In a given area of land that one large farm occupies, many small farms can produce equally, if not more food per acre, with more energy efficiency. It's been proven over and over. If we human beings are to reconnect with the Earth and the life of the Earth, and sustain and heal that life, it is going to mean we need to create smaller farms that the community can have relationships with.

We run what is known as a community-supported agriculture, or CSA, farm. Family members pay a monthly or annual fee and then divide up the weekly allotment that comes from the farm. I view the CSA concept as a completely different economic process than we are used to thinking of traditionally as "market agriculture." Historically, in market agriculture, we can see that the "market" has not maintained its farmer population. If the market system worked for farmers, you would see more of them prospering. [Several jabbering kids hurry by, on the way to their next project. They pass two of their classmates, who are pushing wheelbarrows stacked high with freshly scythed hay.]

When someone goes to the supermarket to buy food, only ten cents or less goes to the farmer. The only way to survive on that is to grow ten times more product, which is not possible without large capital inputs. So farming has become a system run by banks and large industrial corporations, subsidized by our taxes, that keeps food artificially cheap, driving out the small farmer who is not subsidized and can't compete with their prices.

There is no future for the family farm under that system. So we need an approach where the people eating the food work directly with the people growing the food. If we want to create a local agriculture that is not so totally dependent on banks for capital, fossil fuels for energy, toxic chemicals for pest problems, and chemical fertilizers, and not burdened by the environmental destruction that comes from all that, we need to bring it back to a food system that works locally. We will need local farmers who have economic support that can sustain them and respects the Earth. We worked in market agriculture for several years.... We had a small farmers' market locally in Covelo and sold to natural food markets in the county. There were not enough stores for us to be sustainable. We were only able to squeak by on limited income because we were growing all of our own family's meat, milk, and produce. But it was impossible to do any of the capital improvements — build fences, lay pipelines — that we needed to take it to an economically viable level.

In 1988 we heard about the CSA approach. As soon as we heard that idea, we knew that this was the way it should be: having a relationship with the people eating our food rather than a market relationship where we come to market with our produce, get people excited enough to buy something, and have to move the prices around to compete with our neighbor or other growers. In the conventional market the most important thing is that the food is cheap. That's the best deal. But if that means the Earth gets shafted producing it, and the farmer gets shortchanged and disappears, have we really gained any advantage? Farmers become an expendable resource, unrecognized as critically valuable people in the community. When the community supports the farm and farmer directly, then instead of getting ten cents from a dollar spent on the food, the farmer is getting eighty or ninety cents that can really be utilized on the farm. And that makes all the difference in the world to create economic viability. Even going to the farmers' market makes it difficult to *survive because we have to load all the food, get it to the market, sit there and sell it, and if it isn't sold, we have to take it back to the farm. So we're really absorbing some of the middleman's and retailer's costs, which makes it difficult.*

GLORIA: *When we grow for our community members, we aren't looking out in the field of lettuce and thinking, "That's a dollar a head; next week it may be fifty cents a head; what is somebody going to pay for it?" Instead, we are getting away from the idea of what the vegetable costs, and instead we're thinking, "Terry Nieves is going to eat this, Marla Anderson is going to eat this." Their money for that lettuce goes to support the farm, environmentally and socially, and to have a relationship with their food and the farm, to support a farm that invites schoolkids into the farm. Alan Chadwick used to call it "finding your affinity with nature and life." Kids visiting a large corporate farm get to see a farmer drive off in a large tractor on a hundred-acre field — not much to interact with.*

A unique community supports our farm. We have the farmers, the farmers' families, the apprentices, the member families from the Bay Area and Mendocino County, and the plants and animals. We have 180 member families. This is our sixteenth year. Maybe half have been with us the whole time. They have raised and educated their families around the farm, changed their diet, changed their budgets. There are things they don't buy anymore, habits they don't have anymore because they get their basket every week and learn to cook and eat according to what's in season, and they have been thrilled with that — particularly in how that develops their relationship with their children. Many of the families' children come to the farm, make compost, work on the farm, and develop a different relationship with food, and vegetables, and money. When they get their basket, many of the families lay it out on the table and think about what they're going to eat for the next few days.

Some people can't adapt to that of course. They'd rather go to the store or the farmers' market and pick what they want, when they want it, and the quantity they want, and that's perfectly fine. But we want people to be concerned about community and coming to the farm and seeing the farm and working with us and being concerned about the challenges and successes on the farm.

STEPHEN: *We need that flexibility on the farm because we don't know what nature is going to do each year. This year we planted fifteen hundred plants of broccoli and cabbage about three weeks ago, right before the late deluge of rain we had this year. In all the twenty-odd years we've been growing here, that has never happened. We got so much water in an already saturated ground that the rootlets just sat there smothered in water, unable to grow. They're dead! We've never before lost a whole crop like that at one time. In a market format, the farmer is just out of luck at that point. If you are monocropping, with only one crop like corn, instead of a diversified farm of many crops, and you get a bad year where you lose a crop, and you're on a weak economic footing, that can be the end. It can mean the foreclosure of your land. [A parent stops by to ask Gloria when they will need to have the evening meal prepared. Another parent is cutting flowers nearby for the table.]*

Instead, CSAs humanize the economic process. Schumacher called it "economics as if people matter." In the market, everybody is trying to find a new niche, a niche that works — which is great for a year or two until every other farmer finds the same niche, and then it's off to finding another new niche to compete with. In this county, hops were the niche, then it was sheep, then pears for a while, now it's wine grapes. I don't want to constantly fight that process; I simply want to grow good food. And I want to have lots of other farms around us growing good food, too. I don't want to be in competition with them, finding niches or underpricing them. I just want to serve our community, meet their needs, and meet my family's needs out of that relationship.

It takes only 180 households to support a small family farm. This is the opportunity for people today to make real change. Community farms can be initiated by a group of eaters finding a farmer to work with or by a farmer seeking out a group of eaters. We could be much less dependent on fossil fuels from the other side of the world by farming this way locally. By growing a lot of the food that is now coming from other parts of California and the world, we could have a healthy, diversified agriculture that feeds us. Being on the farm helps each of us understand the agricultural process, what our part in it is, and what is healthy for us all in the long run.

There are those who denigrate the sixties and seventies as worthless excursions into mindless hedonism and excoriate the flower children and everything they stood for. The organic food movement and many of the small organic farms we are blessed with started with the flower children dropping out from what was, wanting to live healthier, more peaceful lives. They're the ones who felt the problems, went back to the land, and relearned how to work with nature. And it will be their little islands of sanity and health, some now matured into productive farms through hard work, that will be revealed to have been the better, more sustainable way after all: the poor inheriting the Earth.

Empathy, Community, Care

Full, grassroots democracies based on traditional wisdom and active love for our neighbors will eventually supersede what we find around us now. There is nothing revolutionary about a society that cares enough to fulfill everyone's needs, that honors the rights of everyone to have a livelihood, to be educated and trained, to have health care and dignity in old age. Such is the practice of many other successful, technically advanced cultures and businesses in Europe and elsewhere that we share the Earth with. These are the choices that a responsible, mature, democratic society can make. They are changes we need to make now.

Let me ask you. What is it you want for your children, for your aging parents, for your own daily life with your neighbors here on Earth? Unless you are one of the very few who live in an elite world based on privilege and an unfairly balanced accumulation — the "haves and the have mores"— you most likely will agree that there has to be a better way than the chaos and misery perpetuated by uncaring financial systems, misery that starts with the homeless on the streets of our cities and stretches around the globe to include many millions of the dispossessed and destitute.

The fundamentalist church community I grew up in, despite a belief system I disagreed with, had the strengths that are found in community, especially religious communities. Its members shared a set of values they were passionate about, committed to, and would sacrifice for. There are those, of course, who take this commitment to fanatical extremes, who are willing to kill others who don't accept their belief system, but that doesn't lessen the importance of commitment to values, and of community that can be effectively built around values. Community is a secular form of religion, just as religion is a spiritual form of community, and if we are going to be at all effective in regaining the momentum of caring for each other that is the heart of true democracy, which is threatened now by those who want to destroy its foundations, we must build bridges between those who share the values of caring for each other but who may not share particular belief systems. Tolerance, rather than disdain, is the only way to recover the future, to build community that is inclusive, to bring the Golden Rule back into our neighborhoods and businesses.

Creative Action Heroes

Poets and mystics tell us that our body, our own personal pile of bones and ganglia, is a thing that we use — we ourselves are the using. Our reality is invisible. We are a verb, a process, a function, an action. We *are* our experiencing, we *are* our doing, we *are* our creating.

When our ideas about heroes — bigger-than-life political giants like Gandhi, charismatic leaders like John F. Kennedy, make-believe violent hired guns like 007 — are predefined by cultural agreement, we tend to overlook the everyday heroes around us who are not so obvious. They may be humble and not draw attention to themselves, or the impact they have on other people's lives may not be as dramatic as those in the stories the media serves up to us.

We also tend to fawn over the famous who have somehow stopped screwing up; celebrities, for example, who stop taking drugs after fifteen years are lauded for their newfound self-control. Meanwhile, unsung heroes around us who quietly keep doing what they've always done go unrecognized, unthanked, uncelebrated.

What sets true heroes apart in their actions is their creativity, first in their own lives, and then in the actions they take that make a positive difference in their community and world. It's no longer the lone gun, the charismatic leader, the motivator, the bully, the father figure, the mother figure who is going to get us safely home or even over the next hill. It will be the faithful, the hopeful, the fair, the wise, the courageous, the prudent, the loving — and also the friendly, the reliable, the caring, the positive, the engaged, the participant, the self-responsible, the self-deprecating, the truth-teller, the partner, the team member.

And now I turn to you, those of you whom I have been writing this book about. Look at you! You're everywhere. Some of you are leaders, some are followers; most of you can be either, depending on what is needed. You, our quiet, reliable, behind-the-scenes, everyday heroes, unnoticed, unrecognized, never drawing attention to yourselves, but always, always, always there, cheerfully pulling in your place.

For me, "creative" and "action" are the words I find most commonly associated with you, because without your cheerful creativity and sustained action, your character and heart would not be so easily revealed to us for admiration. Your creative actions are the essence of meaningful work.

The sacred spark that lies within each of us is not owned or controlled by anyone else. It is not confined by someone else's definition of god or religion. It does not ask for permission to create and make things better. It does not seek acceptance or definition by holy books or ancient histories. The sacred spark is ever moving, ever growing, ever creating, ever seeking the higher way of creative action, and it hungers for meaningful work.

The Law of Love

During my transition between the world of corporate work and my work with Cesar Chavez in Delano, I was a volunteer union organizer working on the grape boycott. The farmworkers were seeking contracts that would stop the unfair exploitation of their labor and give them a decent standard of living. Our main tactic at the time was to gather groups of people, make up picket signs, and walk up and down the sidewalk in front of a supermarket waving our signs, singing union songs, chanting and yelling slogans.

Such tactics are confrontational and uncomfortable, but necessary. Poor people who can't buy media time and newspaper ads must rely on giving their time, creating a ruckus, or other means to get attention to their cause. Nonviolence forbids the destruction of property and the harming of people, so other tactics must be employed to offset the power of money and influence that is being challenged. Spiritual tactics — love in action — are employed for social change; truth-telling, imagination, creativity, friendliness, and moral persuasion are tactics that heal and don't destroy. Boycotts are only effective if they are focused and sustained, simple to understand, and supported by enough consumers to cause financial rather than physical pain.

At one point I decided to try a different tactic entirely. I picked out a nearby supermarket, where I would arrive every day by myself at opening time and stand by the door with information leaflets. I didn't shove them at people, or yell at them. I just stood there with my "Boycott Grapes" button, greeting customers with a smile as they arrived to shop. I was doing what the Quakers call "bearing witness": the visible, outward sign of an inward conviction. Over the weeks I became a fixture, the store's "unofficial greeter." I think I was actually building their overall business while I was hurting their grape sales. I would furtively drive through the back after hours to count the number of wooden grape boxes they were throwing out, and it dwindled to almost nothing by the time I moved on. Employees would bring me a cup of coffee and whisper that I was having an effect. I was on a first-name basis with many of the customers who shopped there. It was true one-to-one marketing, lighthearted and fun. Sure, there were a few dour grumblers who never smiled and made caustic comments, and who probably bought grapes just to spite me. But the community held, barriers were dropped, resistances were overcome. Whatever fear some feel when confronted by shouting picket lines was avoided, leaving now the option of a one-to-one relationship, and the possibility that understanding and acceptance could replace intolerance and avoidance. A way had been prepared.

At the end of his wistful last book, *The Law of Love and the Law of Violence*, Leo Tolstoy wrote:

> *Put the good of your life in the progressive liberation of your mind, freedom from all the illusions of the flesh, and in the perfecting of your love for your fellow man — which is in essence the same thing. As soon as you begin to live like this, you will feel a joyous sensation full of liberty and happiness. You will be surprised to find that the same external conditions which caused you such anxiety, and which were far from what you wanted, will not prevent your experiencing the greatest possible happiness.*
>
> *And if you are unhappy — I know that you are — reflect upon what is proposed to you here, which is not the product of my imagination merely, but of the thoughts and feelings of the best minds and hearts. It provides the only way to deliver you from your unhappiness and give you the greatest good you can get in this life.*
>
> *That is what I have wanted to say to you, my brothers [and sisters]. Before I died.*

And just before my dad died, he sat up in bed, looked up into the distance, and said, "It's so beautiful."

Meaningful work comes alive
with love of others as well as ourselves.
And that requires you and me.

epilogue

[local creative action]

We need to honor the saints in our midst. We have to support our small heroes. Who knows, perhaps that's what the twenty-first century has in store for us. The dismantling of the Big. Big bombs, big dams, big ideologies, big contradictions, big countries, big wars, big heroes, big mistakes. Perhaps it will be the Century of the Small.

— Arundhati Roy

Confronting *all* of today's problems is pretty overwhelming, but thankfully *all* of them are not our responsibility. An organic family farmer can shake her head at the tragedy and shame of some politician's decision and feel overcome by the personal tragedies of an unneeded war. She may choose to write letters and protest on a street corner, but her use, her craft, her main job is to grow and harvest the food. She cannot neglect her personal path, her meaningful work, by trying to change every wrong in the world.

By tending her garden, her farm, in her own personal way, which in itself changes the world for good, she is in her place, has grabbed a problem, and is mending it. She is loving us, her community, bright and shining with hope. She is making a difference — and fixing the world.

In every community, every neighborhood, every business, every church can be found unheralded Creative Action Heroes who go about fixing the world rather than escaping it. We can ignore them, and let them continue their quiet, crucial actions without much thanks — what most of them would want anyway because recognition is not why they do it — or we can honor them publicly for who they are and what they do. We can give thanks in public for a job well done, an example to be emulated, a life to be remembered. Who are the real heroes in your community? Here is a fantasy I hope will happen sometime soon, celebrating some of my heroes, real and imagined, in my own community:

Welcome, ladies and gentlemen, to our Second Annual Creative Action Awards. Tonight we are honoring some ordinary people like you and me. These awards are based on mutually shared community values lived out by local heroes doing meaningful work.

Bret and Sid Cooperrider moved here several years ago to help their parents, Els and Allen, recipients of our very first community medal last year. Together the Cooperriders created our community "clubhouse," the Brewpub. With all-organic food from our local farmers and organic beer made on the premises, a community meeting place blossomed. This is where our micro radio station first beamed out to the community. This is where our local organic network was first discussed and then formed and still meets today. We didn't like the standards our federal government was using to certify organic foods, because it was becoming less than organic, so we took it into our own hands and created the Renegade label, following our own community standards, which were much tougher than those of the USDA. We did this to protect the health of our friends and neighbors here in our community and to help the market for our small farmers. The Brewpub is where the idea for banning genetically modified organisms from the county was first discussed and then organized. And who can forget the night we won, when Monsanto and the rest of the chemical bullies were thrown out on their fat wallet butts, and Guitar Shorty led the whole crowd out into the street for an impromptu boogie to celebrate? This is also where our new community credit union was first discussed and organized. This is where we created our alternative Briarpatch Chamber of Commerce, which has organized the ballot initiative to withdraw WalMart's business license for colonizing our county, practicing predatory pricing, and illegally removing community currency to enrich their founders (who are barely getting by on their net worth of $100 billion). Be sure and vote next Tuesday. Good food, good beer, good company. Bret makes the beer and Sid makes the graphics and they both do everything else too, besides making everyone feel welcome. Our Creative Action Hero community medal for our heroes Bret and Sid will now take its honored place in our display here at the Brewpub, up on the mezzanine. We love you guys.

Laura Hamburg is the founder and editor of our community newspaper, the *Bullhorn*. When Laura came back to town after a successful career with a big city newspaper, all we had was our standard small town newspaper, owned by a large corporation located who knows where. It did all the things a newspaper usually does, but it was dull and boring and always writing "down" to us, and it did not represent the whole community. Laura brought passion and care and inclusion and love and a lot of fun to our community. I know the *Bullhorn* offends some of our seniors and business folks now and then, and I'm not going to mention the dustup with Reverend Billy over at the Gospel Tabernacle, but the paper has included a lot more of us in the published conversation, and by opening its website to everyone who has something to say, the vitality of our community has soared. Our Creative Action Hero community medal goes, with our love and honor, to our friend and neighbor and hero Laura "good-ol'-fashioned-tell-it-like-it-is-and-let-the-chips-fall-where-they-may-the-advertisers-be-damned-this-is-not-a-get-rich-scheme-journalist" Hamburg.

Small, local businesses are still the lifeblood of our community, and if we're smart enough, we'll shop less and less at the Big Box Monsters, and more and more at our local stores. Shop the local small businesses that make you smile inside when you think about them because they are fun and lighthearted, and you know the owners, and they offer stuff that is useful and lasts. Like Don's Shoes, where you go for great knowledge and service and Don's caring and integrity. Tonight we are honoring Don not only as a business owner we care about and trust but as an artist and volunteer. His art graces the walls of his store, as well as other businesses in town, and he is often seen collecting and bringing food to the food bank in his old truck. His talents and care add another dimension to the love we have for Don as a person. Our Creative Action Hero community medal goes to Don Hewitt.

Sharon Walker has been our part-time community organizer now for three years. Her other job is managing the all-organic produce department at the co-op, where at least 50 percent of the fruit and vegetables come from local farms. As a community, we decided to tax ourselves to fund a person whose sole job is to organize us to be an effective community that lives our values. The first thing she did was organize our community credit union. It is now accepting deposits, federally insured, that will be used to offer loans to small farmers, so they can build greenhouses and grow food for our community year-round; to homeowners who want to install alternative energy systems; to small, local businesses to expand their services; and to new, local businesses and cooperatives who want to add services to meet our community's needs. The credit union will also be the center for our local community currency operation, Better Bucks. We want the bucks to stop here. Next Sharon organized the alternative Briarpatch Chamber of Commerce, which is now going strong, and she's just returned from the vacation we forced on her. We almost had to tie her up and take her to the plane to get her out of our hair. But, Gawd, do we love this woman. Our hearts are full of gratitude for her energy, and for the community she has helped foster in her own unique way. Our Creative Action Hero community medal goes to Sharon Walker.

We all know that large white building just outside of town, the one we all call "The Corp." Many of us go there often to walk along the creek and wetlands that the company has established on the property and deeded to the conservation district. When they moved their business here five years ago, we were wary of the potential impact they would have on our community. We'd heard all the stories of large companies coming in, paying off the politicians, throwing their weight and money around to get what they want, dominating the community. First, we were surprised by their openness. Not only did they post their financial information on the company's own internal website but they also posted it on their external website for all to see. Profit and loss statements, cash flow, balance sheets, all are updated weekly. They use this information internally for planning, so all employees know how the company is doing and what to adjust, but they are so proud of how they do business and care so much about our community that they want complete transparency. They have nothing to hide and are fiercely proud of their sustainable, ecology-based values. Included are their monthly sustainability reports on their recycling program, the process and costs of handling their waste stream, their donations program (political donations are strictly forbidden), and their Community Crusader Awards Program. They also publish the salaries of their democratically elected management team, and their average wage, for comparison purposes. The other surprise was the company's ownership and board of director structure. Outside investors hold two seats on the board and own one-third of the company. (These investors must reside within the county.) The employees, who also have two seats on the board, own another third. And the company's founders, with their two seats, own the final third. A board president, who comes from the community and is elected by board consensus, holds a final, seventh seat. Tonight we are honoring founder and CEO Sherrie Coughlin for her creative innovations and genuine community care, and with her the president of their employees' union, Raul Rodriguez.

And what can we say about the Decater family that hasn't been said so many times before? Of course, they supply our community with incredibly nutritious and delicious organic food from their Live Power Community Farm up in Round Valley. But we must also mention their efforts to build and sustain community, which has rooted our common identity in what "local" really means. As a member of their farm, I look forward to picking up my weekly box of fresh veggies as Gloria makes her rounds to the drop-off points, and to visiting "our" farm on community weekends to weed and drive the horse team and pretend that I'm a real farmer. We used to use terms like "pillar of the community" and "salt of the earth" to describe people like Stephen and Gloria. By supporting them, our community is anchored in the Earth and its bounty, and the joyful leaping farmer on our Creative Action award celebrates the foundation of any useful community — most importantly, local organic family farms. Our

Creative Action Hero community medal goes with heartfelt fondness and deep, deep love to our heroes Gloria and Stephen Decater.

As we honor the selfless contributions of the Creative Action Heroes who cocreate with us the meaning of our lives and work together, may we each give thanks for these, our friends and neighbors, and the amazing grace that accompanies a responsible, caring community whose members have faith in each other.

The Seven Seeds of Meaningful Work

Meaningful work comes alive
with faith in others as well as ourselves.
And that requires hope....

Meaningful work comes alive
when hope engenders positive change.
And that requires justice....

Meaningful work comes alive
when justice acts from care and compassion.
And that requires temperance....

Meaningful work comes alive
when temperance moderates thoughtless greed.
And that requires prudence....

Meaningful work comes alive
with the prudence of a creative democracy.
And that requires courage....

Meaningful work comes alive
when purposeful courage fits community needs.
And that requires love....

Meaningful work comes alive
with love of others as well as ourselves.
And that requires you and me.

acknowledgments

This book's genesis was a slide show, *Creative Action Heroes*, that I presented in January 2003 at a plenary session of the Eco-Farm conference, an annual gathering of the organic farmers who founded the organic food movement. The presentation was my tribute and thanks to them and their work. My friend, Hal Zina Bennett, saw it and suggested I write a book. He happens to be a successful writer, author, seminar leader, and writing coach, and he introduced me to my publisher, New World Library; my editor, Jason Gardner; and his own book agent, Barbara Deal. I wish every potential author had it as easy as he made it for me to get a start. He somehow failed to mention, though, how difficult it is to write a book and how many hours I would have to devote to it.

Hal coached me by editing the first draft and continuing to give advice. Thank you, Hal, for seeing the potential. Jason Gardner took it from there. By nudging, suggesting, questioning, and encouraging, he skillfully helped me shape it into what it needed to become. Thank you, Jason, for one of the most soul-growing experiences I've ever had. Along the way, Patricia Heinicke Jr. also edited it for clarity and grammar. Thank you, Patricia. Barbara Deal made it possible to get a contract done with no hassles. Thank you, Barbara. And my appreciation and thanks to Marc Allen, Munro Magruder, Kim Corbin, Tona Pearce Myers, Mary Ann Casler, Mike Ashby, and everyone at New World Library, a company that practices many of the ideals suggested in this book.

Jasch and Kathleen Hamilton at Diamond Organics provided a desk and a computer and so much more for use after hours during final writing and editing. When describing meaningful work, it is helpful to be engaged in it with people who care. Jasch, Kathleen, Bruce, Concha, Dora, Elvis, Enrique, Fabiola, Gloyd, Hana, Kathryn, Lauren, Leticia, Luis, Lupe, Maria, Mary Lou, Maxi, Nancy, Ortencia, Samantha, and Steve. Hard work, genuine service, commitment, laughs. What good work should always be.

Thank you all.

notes

Introduction

p. 6   ...*We as a group*...Paul H. Ray, PhD, and Sherry Ruth Anderson, PhD, *The Cultural Creatives* (New York: Harmony Books, 2000).

p. 7   ...*Earth First's Dave Foreman has said*...EcoFuture: "Dave Foreman, a Dialogue with Derrick Jensen," www.ecofuture.org/pk/pkar9510.html.

p. 7   ...*According to a recent* State of the World *report*...*State of the World 2003*, Worldwatch Institute (New York: W. W. Norton & Company, 2003), p. 4.

p. 7   ...*as pointed out by columnist Molly Ivins*...WorkingForChange, Molly Ivins, March 29, 2005, www.workingforchange.com/article.cfm?itemID=18800.

Chapter One: Faith

p. 20   ...*best way to destroy democratic society*...Abraham H. Maslow, *Maslow on Management* (New York: John Wiley & Sons, 1998), p. 82.

p. 21   ...*remaking the "lethal culture" of our elders*...Theodore Roszak, *The Making of a Counter Culture* (Garden City, NY: Anchor Books, 1969), p. 48.

p. 29   ...*not a single mention of Jesus*...Thom Hartmann, *What Would Jefferson Do?* (New York: Harmony Books, 2004), pp. 164–74.

p. 38   ...*There's this great joke*...Laura Miller, "In Heaven's Smoking Section," *Salon* magazine, November 2, 2002, www.salon.com/books/int/2002/11/02/lamott/index3.html.

p. 45   ...*Faith will be defined*...Jim Wallis, *God's Politics* (New York: HarperCollins, 2005), pp. 368–71.

p. 48   ...executives who downplay ethics...www.newss.ksu.edu/WEB/News/NewsReleases/businessresearch101204.html.

Chapter Two: Hope

p. 53 ...*study devoted to a specific type of depression*...Viktor E. Frankl, *Man's Search for Meaning* (New York: Simon & Schuster, 1985), p. 165. Echoed in Wilson Van Dusen, *The Natural Depths in Man* (New York: Harper & Row, 1972), pp. 134–44.

p. 54 ...*If you follow your bliss*...Diane K. Osbon, *The Joseph Campbell Reader* (New York: HarperCollins, 1991), pp. 58–59.

p. 55 ...*The only hypothesis*...Guy Murchie, *The Seven Mysteries of Life* (Boston: Houghton Mifflin, 1978), pp. 621–25.

p. 56 ...*We must be willing to get rid of the life we've planned*...Diane K. Osbon, *The Joseph Campbell Reader* (New York: HarperCollins Publishers, 1991), pp. 18, 19.

p. 56 ...*the prime document of America's third revolution*...Stewart Brand, *The Next Whole Earth Catalog* (Sausalito, CA: Point, 1980), p. 46.

p. 61 ...*We utterly deny all outward wars*...en.wikipedia.org/wiki/Quakers#The_Peace_Testimony.

p. 62 ...*Early in the history of the labor movement*...Robert Lawrence Smith, *A Quaker Book of Wisdom* (New York: Eagle Brook/William Morrow, 1998), pp. 131–33.

p. 64 ...*The mistake of all political doctrines*...Leo Tolstoy, *The Law of Love and the Law of Violence* (New York: Holt, Rinehart and Winston, 1970), pp. 10–11, 27, 77.

p. 71 ...*"Be kind," said the philosopher Philo*...en.wikiquote.org/wiki/Quote_of_the_Day_proposals.

p. 71 ...*one way of taking religion seriously, profoundly, deeply, and earnestly*...Abraham H. Maslow, *Maslow on Management* (New York: John Wiley & Sons, 1998), pp. 83, 103.

p. 75 ...*the potential creator's whole being outstretched*...Edward Matchett, *Creative Action* (London: Turnstone Books, 1975), pp. 38, 58, 59.

p. 76 ...*there is nothing that makes people so generous*...Brenda Ueland, *If You Want to Write* (Saint Paul, MN: Graywolf Press, 1987), p. 179.

p. 77 ...*Chadwick introduced a unique approach*...Martha Brown. 2000. The Farm and Garden projects at the University of California, Santa Cruz. "West of Eden," *Chronicle of the University of California*, Issue 3, 2000, pp. 29-41. http://zzyx.ucsc.edu/casfs/about/fgstory.html.

Chapter Three: Justice

p. 86 ...*That which is known as the Christian religion*...St. Augustine treatise: *Retractt*, I, xiii. Please see "Shadow of the Third Century," by Alvin Boyd Kuhn, PhD, members.tripod.com/~pc93/shadow.htm.

p. 92 ...*When we are really honest with ourselves*...United Farm Workers website: www.ufw.org.

Chapter Four: Temperance

p. 100 ... *The World Values Survey* ... *AdBusters* magazine #51 Jan–Feb 2004. See also World Values Survey, www.worldvaluessurvey.org.

p. 101 ... *It is the little, pathetic attempts* ... Robert Pirsig, *Zen and the Art of Motorcycle Maintenance: An Inquiry into Values* (New York: Bantam Books, 1974), pp. 351–52, 388.

p. 104 ... *We have known workmen who really wanted to work* ... Charles Peguy, *The Choice Is Always Ours*, ed. Dorothy Berkley Phillips, Elizabeth Boyden Howes, and Lucille Nixon (Wheaton, IL: Quest Books, 1975), pp. 377–78.

p. 108 ... *A recent published survey showed that 48 percent* ... aol.careerbuilder.com/share/aboutus/pressreleasesdetail.aspx?id=pr154&sd=1/17/2005&ed=12/31/2005.

p. 108 ... *The phones don't stop* ... Gilbert Neal, "The Phones Don't Stop," *Salon* magazine, April 22, 2005, archive.salon.com/tech/feature/2004/01/08/call_center.

p. 109 ... *something more vital* ... Studs Terkel, *Working* (New York: The New Press, 1972, 1974), pp. 244, 266, 340, 343, 355.

p. 110 ... *the path to human happiness* ... Abraham H. Maslow, *Maslow on Management* (New York: John Wiley & Sons, 1998).

p. 110 ... *Theory X and Theory Y behavior* ... Gary Heil, Warren Bennis, Deborah C. Stephens, Douglas McGregor, *Revisited: Managing the Human Side of the Enterprise* (New York: John Wiley & Sons, 2000).

p. 111 ... *The best, most efficient, most profitable way* ... Jack Stack, *The Great Game of Business* (New York: Doubleday, 1992), pp. 71, 72.

p. 112 ... *Even though research has well proven that companies with good values are more profitable* ... Marjorie Kelly, *Business Ethics*, Winter 2004, pp. 4, 5.

p. 115 ... *live with joy in the cracks* ... *The Briarpatch Book* (San Francisco: New Glide Publications, 1978), p. viii.

p. 119 ... *A civilization built on renewable resources* ... E. F. Schumacher, *Small Is Beautiful: Economics as If People Mattered* (New York: Harper & Row, 1973), p. 137.

p. 119 ... *Buddhist economics must be very different* ... E. F. Schumacher, *Small Is Beautiful* (New York: Harper & Row, 1973), p. 52.

Chapter Five: Prudence

p. 125 ... *88 percent of all new job creation* ... Thom Hartmann, *Unequal Protection* (Emmaus, PA: Rodale, 2002), p. 267.

p. 125 ... *a typical CEO earns eight to ten times* ... www.faireconomy.org/press/2004/EE2004_pr.html.

p. 126 ... *Britain will this year export* ... www.isec.org.uk/articles/reclaiming.html.

p. 127 ... *After more than a decade of advocating* ... Marjorie Kelly, *The Divine Right of Capital* (San Francisco: Berrett-Kohler, 2001), pp. xii, 173.

p. 128 ...*[W]hat is needed is a foundational change*...Thom Hartmann, *Unequal Protection* (Emmaus, PA: Rodale, 2002), p. 252.

p. 128 ...*History tells us that when corporate power is unrestrained*... "BuzzFlash Interview with Thom Hartmann: Why WalMart Is Not a Person," Working forChange website, www.workingforchange.com/article.cfm?itemID=18459.

p. 134 ...*there is but one social responsibility for corporate executives*... www.colorado.edu/studentgroups/libertarians/issues/ friedman-soc-resp-business.html.

p. 134 ...*If you find an executive*...Joel Bakan, *The Corporation* (New York: Free Press / Simon & Schuster, 2004), pp. 34–35, 252.

p. 135 ...*Curaçao citizens organize a campaign*... "Behind the Shine: The Other Shell Report, 2003," ww.foe.co.uk/resource/reports/behind_shine.pdf.

p. 135 ...*Bayer's GE [genetically engineered] crop herbicide Finale*...*The Japan Times*, December 7, 2004.

p. 135 ...*Infant death rates*...www.mothersalert.org/tooth3.html.

p. 135 ...*An unprecedented joint statement*...Steve Connor, "G8 Scientists Tell Bush: Act Now — or Else..." *The Independent*, June 8, 2005, news.independent.co.uk/world/science_technology/story.jsp?story =645071.

p. 135 ...*Fifty-five thousand people have likely died*...Tony Pugh, "Vioxx Deaths: Maybe 55,000," *Wichita Eagle*, November 19, 2004, www.kansas.com/mld/eagle/living/health/10220598.htm.

p. 136 ...*More than 5 million children alive*... "Overview: The Global Crisis," Campaign for Tobacco-Free Kids website, tobaccofreekids.org/ campaign/global/crisis.shtml.

p. 136 ...*Nearly 95 percent*...Michael Scherer, "Make Your Taxes Disappear," *Mother Jones*, March–April 2005, www.motherjones.com/news/feature/ 2005/03/corporate_tax_bill.html.

p. 136 ...*Corporations can live forever*...*The Hightower Lowdown* newsletter, vol. 5, no. 4.

p. 141 ...*When visitors learn that our economic success requires*...Ricardo Semler, *The Seven-Day Weekend* (New York: Penguin Group, 2003), pp. 9, 19, 31.

p. 141 ...*Organization Chart*...:Ricardo Semler, *Maverick* (New York: Warner Books, 1993), appendix B.

p. 149 ...*The Cooperative Corporation itself is a moral entity*...Greg MacLeod, *From Mondragon to America* (Sydney, Nova Scotia, Canada: Cape Breton University Press, 1997), p. 89.

p. 153 ...*My company's technologies*...Ray Anderson, *Mid-Course Correction* (White River Junction, VT: Chelsea Green Publishing, 1998), pp. 5, 89.

p. 154 ...*Stewardship is defined as the willingness*...Peter Block, *Stewardship* (San Francisco: Berrett-Koehler, 1993), pp. xx, xxii, 43, 7.

p. 159 ...*democracy as a way of life*...John Dewey, "Creative Democracy," www.beloit.edu/~pbk/dewey.html.

Chapter Six: Courage

p. 164 ...*Myth One — Industrial Agriculture Will Feed the World*...Andrew Kimbrell, *Fatal Harvest* (Sausalito, CA: Foundation for Deep Ecology, 2002).

p. 165 ...*This is the true joy of life*...www.quotationspage.com/quote/27168.html.

p. 167 ...*According to extensive research*...The New Farm Field Trials, Rodale Institute, www.newfarm.org/depts/NFfield_trials/1003/carbonsequest.shtml.

p. 167 ...*According to the largest review yet*...James Randerson, "Organic Farming Boosts Biodiversity," *New Scientist*, October 11, 2004, quoted in http://www.organicconsumers.org/organic/biodiversity101404.cfm.

p. 172 ...*Women now run almost 15 percent of American farms*...Julia Moskin, "Farm to Market: Women Find Their Place in the Field," *New York Times*, sec. F, p. 1 , June 1, 2005.

p. 174 ...*Small farms almost always produce far more*...Andrew Kimbrell, *Fatal Harvest* (Sausalito, CA: Foundation for Deep Ecology, 2002), p. 57.

p. 175 ...*Felipe Franco was born with no limbs*...Susan Ferriss and Ricardo Sandoval, *The Fight in the Fields: Cesar Chavez and the Farmworkers Movement* (Orlando, FL: Harcourt Brace & Co,), p. 238.

p. 176 ...*According to the most recent tally*...Sandra Steingraber, *Living Downstream* (New York: Vintage Books, 1997), p. 270.

p. 178 ...*Lawn care pesticides are easily absorbed*...www.beyondpesticides.org/photostories/week_1/week_1.htm, www.usga.org/turf/green_section_record/2005/jan_feb/Inorganic.html.

p. 181 ...*In the past 10 years, more than $100 million*...Paul Rogers, "Strawberry Farmers Face Methyl Bromide Showdown," *San Jose Mercury News*, February 9, 2005.

p. 183 ...*My heroes remain the growing legend of organic farmers*...Jesse Ziff Cool, *Your Organic Kitchen* (Emmaus, PA: Rodale, 2000), p. 11.

p. 185 ...*Researchers in Italy found*...Marian Burros, "Is Organic Food Provably Better?" *New York Times*, July 16, 2003.

p. 186 ...*Nine metals found in fertilizers, like arsenic and lead*...Matthew Shaffer, "Wastelands: The Threat of Toxic Fertilizer," U.S. PIRG website, www.pirg.org/toxics/reports/wastelands.

p. 187 ...*which then destroys 97 percent*..."Microwaving Kills Health Benefits," *Journal of the Science of Food and Agriculture*, October 17, 2003, www.soci.org/SCI/pressoffice/2003/html/pr234.jsp.

Chapter Seven: Love

p. 204 ...*Aren't we privileged to live in a time*...www.grannyd.com/speeches.php?id=16&action=list.

p. 220 ...*Put the good of your life in the progressive liberation*...Leo Tolstoy, *The Law of Love and the Law of Violence* (New York: Holt, Rinehart and Winston, 1970), p. 101.

suggested reading and resource links

"What does it profit a man if he gains the whole world and loses his own soul?" The wealth available in libraries and bookstores, especially from small publishers and presses, supercedes, by far, any possible worldly material gains.

Salvation can come from many sources: we can be reborn once, twice, countless times during a lifetime of learning, changing, growing, and doing. My bachelor's degree in liberal arts and literature was attained from the University of Kepler's Paperback Bookstore in Menlo Park, California, founded by pacifist Roy Kepler. I got my master's degree in traditional wisdom and spirituality from the late, great East West Bookstore, also of Menlo Park, and the Seed Center, in the back of Plowshares Bookstore, late of Palo Alto, with a double minor in nonviolence at the Institute for the Study of Non-Violence founded by Joan Baez and Ira Sandperl, late of Palo Alto, and in community activism as part of the United Farm Workers Union, founded by Cesar and Helen Chavez, and Dolores Huerta, of Delano and Keene, California. All course work completed on the job toward a master's in business administration. Enclosed is the dissertation.

Books of wisdom save my soul. To live and work from what's experienced and learned saves my life — born again daily.

Faith [True Belief]

J. B. Phillips – *Your God Is Too Small*
C. S. Lewis – *The Great Divorce*
Leo Tolstoy – *My Confession*
E. F. Schumacher – *A Guide for the Perplexed*
Ralph Waldo Emerson – *Essential Writings*
William James – *Varieties of Religious Experience*
Aldous Huxley – *The Perennial Philosophy*
Phillips, Howes, Nixon – *The Choice Is Always Ours*
Eric Hoffer – *The True Believer*
Thomas Jefferson – *The Jefferson Bible*
John Dominic Crossan – *Jesus: A Revolutionary Biography*
Huston Smith – all his books

Erich Fromm – all his books
Tom Harpur – all his books
Monica Sjoo and Barbara Mor – *The Great Cosmic Mother*
Helen Ellerbe – *The Dark Side of Christian History*
Karen Armstrong – *A History of God*
Alvin Boyd Kuhn – *Shadow of the Third Century*
Susan Jacoby – *Freethinkers*
Robert Ingersoll – *Best of Robert Ingersoll*
Elaine Pagels – *Beyond Belief*
Anne Lamott – *Traveling Mercies*
Jim Wallis – *God's Politics*
The Fundamentalism Project – *Fundamentalisms Comprehended*
Center for Progressive Christianity – www.tcpc.org
Christian Alliance for Progress – www.christianalliance.org

Hope [Soul School]

Leo Tolstoy – *The Kingdom of God Is Within You*
Leo Tolstoy – *Lift Up Your Eyes*
Dorothy Day – *The Long Loneliness*
Thomas Merton – *Thoughts in Solitude*
Evelyn Underhill – *Practical Mysticism*
Carl Jung – *Modern Man in Search of a Soul*
Viktor E. Frankl – *Man's Search for Meaning*
James Hillman – *The Soul's Code*
Joseph Campbell – *Thou Art That*
Hermann Hesse – *Steppenwolf*
J. Krishnamurti – *Think On These Things*
Stephen Mitchell – *Tao Te Ching*
Ken Wilber – *Transformations of Consciousness*
Hazrat Inayat Khan – *The Inner Life*
Robert Thurman – *Inner Revolution*
Guy Murchie – *The Seven Mysteries of Life*
Wilson Van Dusen – *The Natural Depths in Man*
Eknath Easwaran – *God Makes the Rivers to Flow*
Michael Talbot – *The Holographic Universe*
Eckhart Tolle – *The Power of Now*

Justice [Action Heroes]

Mohandas Gandhi – *All Men Are Brothers*
Louis Fischer – *The Life of Mahatma Gandhi*
Henry David Thoreau – *Civil Disobedience*

Martin Luther King Jr. – *A Testament of Hope*
Thomas Jefferson – *The Papers of Thomas Jefferson*
Saul Alinsky – *Reveille for Radicals*
David Harris – *Goliath*
Joan Baez – *And a Voice to Sing With*
Rachel Carson – *Silent Spring*
Sandra Steingraber – *Living Downstream*
Thomas Paine – all his books
Edward Abbey – all his books
Thom Hartmann – all his books
Derrick Jensen – all his books
Arundhati Roy – all her books
Howard Zinn – *A People's History of the United States*
Bill Hicks – *Love All the People*
Robert Wolff – *Original Wisdom*
John Perkins – *Confessions of an Economic Hit Man*
Jacques E. Levy – *Cesar Chavez*
Peter Matthiessen – *Sal Si Puedes*
The Federalist Papers – www.law.ou.edu/hist/federalist
Conscientious Objectors – www.objector.org
Amy Goodman – www.democracynow.org
Juan Cole – www.juancole.com
Antiwar.com – www.antiwar.com
Truthout – www.truthout.org
Common Dreams – www.commondreams.org
Mother Jones magazine – www.motherjones.com
Yes magazine – www.yesmagazine.org
Utne Reader – www.utne.com

Temperance [The Briarpatch Way]

E. F. Schumacher – *Small Is Beautiful*
Stewart Brand – *The Whole Earth Catalog*
Stewart Brand – *CoEvolution Quarterly*
Briarpatch – *The Briarpatch Book*
Henry David Thoreau – *Walden*
Michael Phillips – *The Seven Laws of Money*
Studs Terkel – *Working*
Aldous Huxley – *Ends and Means*
Philip Slater – *Wealth Addiction*
Warren Johnson – *Muddling Toward Frugality*
David Suzuki – *The Sacred Balance*
Theodore Roszak – *The Making of a Counter Culture*
Charles A. Reich – *The Greening of America*

Helen and Scott Nearing – *Living the Good Life*
Francis Moore Lappé – *Diet for a Small Planet*
Henry Miller – *Stand Still Like a Hummingbird*
Briarpatch Network – www.Briarpatch.net
Briarpatch Co-op – www.briarpatchcoop.com
Manas: The Journal of Intelligent Idealism – www.manasjournal.org
AdBusters magazine – www.AdBusters.org
The Sun magazine – www.theSunMagazine.org
The Ecologist magazine – www.TheEcologist.org
Orion magazine – www.OrionOnline.org
Co-op America – www.coopamerica.org
Grist magazine – www.grist.org
WorkingForChange – www.workingforchange.com

Prudence [Reclaiming the Soul of Business]

Abraham H. Maslow – *Maslow on Management*
Douglas McGregor – *The Human Side of Enterprise*
Peter Block – *Stewardship*
David C. Korten – *When Corporations Rule the World*
Thom Hartmann – *Unequal Protection*
Marjorie Kelly – *The Divine Right of Capital*
Joel Bakan – *The Corporation*
Robert Pirsig – *Zen and the Art of Motorcycle Maintenance*
Keshavan Nair – *A Higher Standard of Leadership*
Max DePree – *Leadership Jazz*
Max DePree – *Leadership Is an Art*
Lewis Richmond – *Work as Spiritual Practice*
Credit Union National Association – www.cuna.org
National Cooperative Business Assoc. – www.ncba.coop
David Batstone – www.rightreality.com
IdealsWork – www.idealswork.com
Worthwhile magazine – www.worthwhilemag.com
Business Ethics magazine – www.business-ethics.com

Courage [Creative Action Heroes]

Wendell Berry – all his books
Vandana Shiva – all her books
Gene Logsdon – all his books
Joseph Campbell – all his books
Andrew Kimbrell – *Fatal Harvest*
Edward Matchett – *Creative Action*

Brenda Ueland – *If You Want to Write*
Steven Pressfield – *The War of Art*
Jesse Ziff Cool – *Your Organic Kitchen*
John Jeavons – *How to Grow More Vegetables*
John E. Ikerd – www.ssu.missouri.edu/faculty/jikerd/papers
Els Cooperrider – www.mendocinorenegade.com
Charles Martin – www.mendocinoorganicnetwork.com
Stephen and Gloria Decater – www.localharvest.org/farms/M32
Jim Cochran – www.swantonberry.com
Ecological Farming Association – www.eco-farm.org
Local Harvest – www.localharvest.org
CSA Farm Directory – www.csacenter.org
Acres USA – www.acresusa.com
The Center for Agroecology – zzyx.ucsc.edu/casfs
Wild Farm Alliance – www.wildfarmalliance.org
International Society for Ecology and Culture – www.isec.org.uk
Pesticide Action Network – www.panna.org
Pesticide Education Network – www.pesticides.org
Beyond Pesticides – www.beyondpesticides.org
Organic Consumers Association – www.organicconsumers.org
Organic Valley Co-op – www.organicvalley.com
Newman's Own Organics – www.newmansownorganics.com
Mountain Valley Growers – www.mountainvalleygrowers.com
Seeds of Change – www.seedsofchange.com
Diamond Organics – www.diamondorganics.com
Organic To Go – www.organictogo.com
Organic Bouquet – www.organicbouquet.com

Love [Useful You]

Leo Tolstoy – *The Law of Love and the Law of Violence*
Leo Tolstoy – *The Death of Ivan Ilych*
bell hooks – *The Will to Change*
Doc Lew Childre – *The HeartMath Solution*
Dean Ornish – *Love and Survival*

permission
acknowledgments

Grateful acknowledgment is given to these publishers and copyright holders for permission to reprint the following quotations in *To Be of Use*:

"The History of the Farm and Gardens Projects at the University of California, Santa Cruz," by Martha Brown, reprinted by permission of the Chronicle of the University of California, http://zzyx.ucsc.edu/casfs/about/fgstory.html.

The poem "to be of use" by Marge Piercy, from *Circles on the Water* (Copyright © 1982 by Marge Piercy) is reprinted by permission of Alfred A. Knopf, a division of Random House, Inc.

"The Semco Survival Manual" by Ricardo Semler, from *Maverick: The Success Story Behind the World's Most Unusual Workplace* (Copyright © 1995 by Ricardo Semler) is reprinted by permission of Warner Books.

index

about the author

Sustainable business pioneer Dave Smith has been an executive assistant to Cesar Chavez, a cofounder of Briarpatch Natural Foods Co-op in Menlo Park, California, and cofounder of gardening company Smith & Hawken. He has held leadership positions in such companies as Real Goods, SelfCare, Seeds of Change, and Diamond Organics and has been a key figure in the organic food movement. A serial startup entrepreneur, Smith cofounded Organic Bouquet, the first national organic floral company, and is currently part of the team introducing Organic To Go, a chain of restaurants offering organic meals for take-out and delivery. He has served on the boards of directors of Ecology Action and Ukiah Natural Foods Co-op in Mendocino County, California, and is a cofounder of Mendocino Organic Network, an alliance of farmers and consumers promoting local, organic, and sustainable farming. His website is www.tobeofuse.com.